Discovering Fife

Already published:
Discovering Galloway
Discovering Lewis and Harris
Discovering West Lothian

Forthcoming:
Discovering Aberdeenshire
Discovering Ayrshire
Discovering East Lothian
Discovering Inverness-shire

Discovering Fife

RAYMOND LAMONT-BROWN

JOHN DONALD PUBLISHERS LTD
EDINBURGH

For Moira

John Donald Publishers Ltd.,
138 St Stephen Street, Edinburgh, EH3 5AA.

ISBN 0 85976 204 1

Phototypeset by Newtext Composition Ltd., Glasgow.
Printed in Great Britain by Bell & Bain Ltd., Glasgow.

Acknowledgements

Raymond Lamont-Brown would like to thank the following for their help in compiling this book:

The Deputy Director of Administration of Dunfermline District Council.

Fife Regional Council, Planning Dept., Information Service.

Fife Forestry District.

Chief Inspector Alistair McLuckie, College Staff Officer for Commandant, Scottish Police College, Tulliallan Castle.

Anthony R. Worner M.V.O., Staff Public Relations Officer, Scotland and Northern Ireland, Maritime Headquarters, Pitreavie.

Mrs Ann Watters, Kirkcaldy Civic Society and the Markinch Centre.

W.D.F. Grant, Area Civil Engineer, ScotRail.

Reverend Mother Prioress, Carmelite Monastery, Dysart.

Brevet Colonel Sir John Gilmour, Bart., D.S.O., T.D.

Margaret Anderson, Entertainment & Tourist Officer, Kirkcaldy District Council.

Tom Johnston, Public Relations Officer, Glenrothes Development Corporation.

David M. Hyman, Community Relations Officer, RAF Leuchars.

By the same author
History of St Mark's Church, Dewsbury
A Book of Epitaphs
Clarinda: The Intimate story of Agnes Maclehose and Robert Burns
Doncaster Rural District
Letters on Witchcraft and Demonology by Sir Walter Scott
Robert Burns's Commonplace Book
A Book of Superstitions
A Book of Proverbs
A Book of Witchcraft
Charles Kirkpatrick Sharpe's Witchcraft in Scotland
Phantoms of the Sea
General Trade in Berwick-upon-Tweed
Robert Burns's Tour of the Borders
The Magic Oracles of Japan
Robert Burns's Tour of the Highlands and Stirlingshire
A New Book of Epitaphs
A Casebook of Military Mystery
Epitaph Hunting
Growing up with the Highland Clans
Scottish Epitaphs
Lothian and the Southeast Borders: Walks for Motorists
Phantoms of the Theatre
My Fun Book of Scotland
East Anglian Epitaphs
Mary, Queen of Scots
Mysteries and Legends
Drives around Edinburgh
Drives around Glasgow
A Visitor's Guide to St Andrews
Mothers-in-Law
A Book of British Eccentrics
Irish Grave Humour

With Peter Adamson
Victorian and Edwardian Fife from Old Photographs
The Victorian and Edwardian Borderland from Rare Photographs
Victorian and Edwardian Dundee and Broughty Ferry from Rare Photographs
Victorian and Edwardian Perthshire from Rare Photographs
Fife Portrait of a County 1910-1950 from Rare Photographs
St Andrews City of Change
Victorian and Edwardian Angus from Rare Photographs

Contents

Enjoying Fife

There are scores of reasons for turning off the M90 and entering the old Kingdom of Fife. Castles, abbeys, woodland walks, safe play areas, clean beaches, water sports, festivals and museums are just fringe benefits, for Fife is full of pleasant surprises of scenery, local crafts and entertainment. Then there are the people, and a more hospitable, individualistic, characterful, enterprising and progressive society does not exist anywhere.

The chapters in this volume on the warm-hearted Kingdom of Fife have been planned so that the places mentioned can be visited in sections to suit touring plans – bit by bit, or as a round trip by whatever transportation is found convenient. But first a few vital statistics: Fife has a population of just over 344,000 in around 117,000 households. From Fife Ness to the extreme south-west, Fife measures 41½ miles, and its breadth from Burntisland to Newburgh is 21 miles. Fife's coastline takes in some 115 miles and its landward boundary is around 61 miles, all enclosing an area of 505 square miles. Indeed the county is growing in landmass for recently the Secretary of State for Scotland added 132 hectares to Fife (from Tayside) to facilitate open-cast coal development.

Fife's regional boundary begins almost in the centre of the river Forth just west of Kincardine Bridge; it heads northeast for Kilbagie and meanders on to turn right at Cult Hill to make a dash round the north edge of Loch Glow and plough through Blairadam Forest to cross the M90 at Keltybridge. It then turns north again to Benarty Hill and east to Auchmuirbridge; then northwest to Butterwell and Burnside to turn east along the Carmore Burn just south of Newton of Balcanquhal. Turning north for Pitmedden Forest, the boundary skirts to the west of Newburgh and meets the Tay at the South Deep, west of Mugdrum Island.

Fife has a diversified countryside of rolling hills; to the west and north lie the Ochils which enter Fife from Perthshire and run on to Newburgh and Tayport. To the east rise the Lomonds which roughly divide Fife into West and East. There are no lofty mountains in Fife and the principal hills include: Kellie Law (557 ft); Largo Law (965 ft); Norman's Law (850 ft); East Lomond (1471 ft); West Lomond (1713 ft); Knock Hill (1189 ft); Saline Hill (1178 ft); and Benarty Hill (1167 ft). Once these hills gave rise to weather lore:

> When Largo Law the mist doth bear,
> Let Kellie Law for storms prepare.

And:

> When Falkland Hill puts on his cap
> The Howe o'Fife will get a drap.

The old kingdom's two main rivers are the Leven, which enters the Firth at Largo Bay and the Eden which runs through the Howe of Fife to enter the North Sea at St Andrews Bay.

In terms of geology, the northlands of Fife, stretching some fifteen miles inland along the Firth of Tay to Newburgh, are mostly basalt and andesite of the Carboniferous and Lower Old Red Sandstone Age; with a volcanic conglomerate around Auchtermuchty. Along the valley of the Eden to its source just outside Fife is sedimentary rock of the Old Red Sandstone Age. Round the coast from St Andrews to Elie it is calciniferous sandstone of the late Carboniferous period. South of the Eden valley to the sea, and east to west from Ceres to Kincardine is a parallelogram of carboniferous rock, ranging from the barren red coal measures around Kirkcaldy to the calcinferous sandstone inland of Inverkeithing.

Regarding administration, Fife is controlled by Fife Regional Council with its regional headquarters in Glenrothes, Dunfermline District Council, Kirkcaldy District Council, North-East Fife District Council, Glenrothes Development Corporation and various community councils. There are five parliamentary constituencies, namely, Dunfermline East, Dunfermline West, Fife Central, Kirkcaldy and North-East Fife; and the region falls within the European Parliament as 'Mid Scotland and Fife'.

The Queen's representative in Fife is the Lord Lieutenant. His chief duties consist in the recommendation for the appointment of magistrates, the appointment of deputy lieutenants and the raising of the militia if needs be in time of civil riot or invasion. The office is largely ceremonial. *All of the places mentioned in the text can be located on the Ordance Survey Maps 58, 59, 65 and 66 on the 1:50,000 scale series.*

Enjoying Fife through . . . Reading

Background reading can add much to the enjoyment of Fife and can be appreciated at a number of levels. There are books on Fife to read before a trip is taken, to prepare for the experience of the old county; books to read while touring, to help exploit local knowledge; and books to enjoy when the suitcase is unpacked and the traveller is home.

Among the largely out-of-print books to look for in public libraries the following can be recommended: Sir Robert Sibbald's *The History, ancient and modern of the Sheriffdoms of Fife and Kinross,* published in Edinburgh in 1710, is a classic work, but easier to read is A.H. Millar's *Fife: Pictorial and Historical* (Westwood, Cupar 1895) which is a two-volume study of people, burghs, castles and mansions up to the late years of Victoria's reign. To these can be added J. Wilkie's *Bygone Fife North of the Lomonds* (1938), T.G. Snoddy's *Afoot in Fife* (1950), J. Geddie's *The Fringes of Fife* (1927) and Theo Lang's *The Kingdom of Fife* (1951).

For local history of burghs and villages in greater detail these are the main works:

Cunningham, A.S. *Inverkeithing, North Queensferry, Rosyth and Naval Base.* (1903)
Stephen, Rev W. *History of Inverkeithing and Rosyth.* (1921)
Marshall, D. *L'île des Chevaux: The Story of Inchkeith.* (1983)
Reid, A. *Kinghorn.* (1906)
Robertson, M. *Old Dunfermline.* (1979)
Muir, A. *The Fife Coal Co Ltd.* (1946)
Holman, R. *History of Cowdenbeath.* (1941)
Centenary Booklet, Lochgelly Burgh. (1977)
Houston, A.McN. *Auchterderran.* (1924)
Young, W. *Cardenden.*
Webster, J.M. *History of Carnock.* (1938)
Culross. National Trust for Scotland. (1985)
Kirkcaldy in a Nutshell. Kirkcaldy Civic Society.
Coaltown of Wemyss. Wemyss Environmental Education Centre. (1983)

Walker, B. & Ritchie, G. *Exploring Scotland's Heritage: Fife and Tayside.* (1987)
Cunningham, A.S. *Rambles in the Parishes of Scoonie and Wemyss.* (1905)
Rankin, F. *Auld Buckhyne* (1986)
Findlay, A.M. *Kennoway, its History and Legends.* (1946)
Milton of Balgonie. Balgonie Primary School. (1986)
Ferguson, K. *A History of Glenrothes.* (1982)
Kettle: Village and Parish Survey. Kettle Primary School. (1984)
Springfield: Village and History. Springfield Primary School. (1984)
Lister, D. & Gillies, J. *Largo Kirk.*
Tayport: Tayport Community Council. (1985)
Laing, A. *Lindores Abbey and the Burgh of Newburgh.* (1876)
Seed, N. *Strathkinness.* (1986)
Lamont-Brown, R. & Adamson, P. *St Andrews: City of Change.* (1984)

These give some idea of the range of books available, and the public libraries offer local collections on each area. Dunfermline District Libraries are particularly to be congratulated on the selection of free booklets they offer on local history, such a title as *Everyday Life in Dunfermline in the late 18th century* being a good example. The Education Centre at East Wemyss Primary School also offers leaflets and study booklets on Fife and their catalogue may be obtained from Basement Suite, East Wemyss Primary School, East Wemyss, by post or by personal call during office hours.

Alas, very few local authorities or companies produce 'town guides', in the old accepted sense, but there are a few such guides extant on Cupar, St Andrews, Dunfermline and Glenrothes.

Enjoying Fife through . . . Reconnoitring

Nature Walks, Heritage Trails, Tourist Routes and Town Walks all offer the visitor a chance to study Fife at a more leisurely pace than motoring. A wide range of leaflets on activity suggestions for Fife are available in the ancient kingdom's *information centres:* The main centres are located at: South Street, LEVEN; 4 Kirkgate, BURNTISLAND; The

Esplanade, KIRKCALDY; The Town House, KIRKCALDY; South Street, ST ANDREWS; Fluthers Car Park, CUPAR (Seasonal); Glen Bridge Car Park, DUNFERMLINE (Seasonal); and at the FORTH ROAD BRIDGE. The Motorway Service Area at KINROSS (on the M90) also has an information centre with data relevant to Fife.

Nature trails can be found at Pittencrieff Park, Ravenscraig, Dunnikier . . . all at Kirkcaldy; Letham Glen, Leven; Tentsmuir Forest; Blairadam Forest; Craighall Den; Cambo and Ladybank.

Look out too for the signposted tourist routes with their distinctive logos; these routes have been worked out by Fife Regional Council to offer the visitor the best in coastal and country tourist routes. And from Rosyth to the Tay Bridge, via the coast of the Firth of Forth, the East Neuk and St Andrews, is set out the Fishing Heritage Trail offering year-round facilities.

Enjoying Fife through . . . Reflecting

'What is this life if, full of care, we have no time to stand and stare': so wrote the 'tramp poet' W.H. Davies (1871-1940), and reflecting on Fife people and their history offers much of interest. Historical classical sources show us that modern Fife was occupied in the early centuries by a Celtic tribe called the *Venicones,* who with the *Vacomagi,* formed a confederation mentioned by the Roman historian Cassius Dio Cocceianus (c.A.D. 150-235) as the *Maeatae.* They constituted a people known as Proto-Picts who were recognised for their metalwork. The lack of permanent Roman installations in Fife, following the conquest of Scotland by Gnaeus Julius Agricola during AD 78-84, would suggest that the *Venicones* were philo-Roman.

The Romans first moved into Fife in AD 82, and after the commencement of the governship of Antoninus Pius, c.A.D. 138, a necklet of forts were constructed from the Forth to the Tay effectively protecting the peninsula of Fife. By AD 170 the Romans abandoned the area. In AD 209 the imperial task force of Emperor Septimius Severus moved into Scotland, and the Romans began construction of the half-legionary fortress at Carpow (near modern Newburgh), to be used by the II and

VIth Legions.

The term *Picti* (Lat: painted) only appears in classical writing from the end of the third century, but by the time that the tribesmen were ravaging the territory north of Hadrian's Wall in the great raid of AD 367, the Picts were a fully developed entity. Legend tells us that the first king of the Picts was Cruithne and that his seven sons gave their names to the regions of Pictland. From one such regional kingdom, *Fib*, comes today's Fife. In the mid-9th century the area we know as Fife was divided into two with a line roughly from Leven to Auchtermuchty – to the west was *Forthrif* and to the east was *Fib.* In Pictish times, Fife's area included Perthshire as far as the Ochils and had its capital at *Kinrimund* (St Andrews); and until the 14th century it included Kinross. Fife is mentioned for the first time, it seems, by St Columba (521-97) as a province of Pictavia. Today the Picts are remembered in Fife through dozens of place names and their homes and fortresses are everywhere; for instance Clatchard's Craig, a multivaleate Iron Age fort near modern Newburgh, was an important Pictish settlement.

In time the throne of Pictland was annexed by Kenneth McAlpin, the Scottish King, and by 850 the Picts had ceased to remain as an independent power. The new Kingdom of Alba, of which the area of modern Fife was a part, had its capital at Scone. From here the web of political and ecclesiastical power spread and Fife was colonised in a religious sense at such sites as St Andrews. By the 12th century there was a royal reform of the kingdom and burghs began to be founded and settlements at such places as Pittenween, Dunfermline and St Monans were to assure Fife's continued importance down the centuries.

From medieval times Fife enjoyed a high standard of living, from the well-watered howes (Vales) of Eden, Leven and Ore, to the low-lying margins of Firth and Tay, to the moors burned to submission for the graising of sheep and stock cattle. As the historian George Buchanan (1506-1582) was to say, Fife was 'a district provided within its own bounds with all things necessary for the use of life', to which subsequent visitors and commentators added remarks on the lush farms, doocots, fisheries and rural scenery.

Today even the fast vanishing aspects of industrial Fife offer interest to the visitor, for once Fife was 'happy in collieries . . . blest in manufactures . . .', as Thomas Pennant recorded in 1772. All these reflections of Fife's history are recorded in her sixteen museums which are a must for the tourist package as they all offer something different. Here they are . . .

Dunfermline District Museum, Viewfield Terrace, Dunfermline.

Pittencrieff House Museum, Pittencrief Park, Dunfermline.

Andrew Carnegie Birthplace Museum, Moodie Street, Dunfermline.

Inverkeithing Museum, Queen Street, Inverkeithing.

Kirkcaldy Museum and Art Gallery, War Memorial Gardens, Kirkcaldy.

Kirkcaldy Industrial Museum, War Memorial Gardens, Kirkcaldy.

McDouall Stuart Museum, Rectory Lane, Dysart.

Buckhaven Museum, Buckhaven Library, College Street, Buckhaven.

Burntisland Museum, Burntisland Library, High Street, Burntisland.

Leven Museum, Leven Library, South Street, Leven.

The Scottish Fisheries Museum & Aquarium, St Ayles, Harbourhead, Anstruther.

Crail Museum & Heritage Centre, Marketgate, Crail.

Fife Folk Museum, Old High Street, Ceres.

Laing Museum, High Street, Newburgh.

The St Andrews Preservation Trust Museum, 12 North Street, St Andrews.

St Andrews University Archaeological Museum, Swallowgate Building, The Scores, St Andrews. And from time to time the *Crawford Centre for the Arts* put on historical displays at their 93 North Street, St Andrews, premises.

Enjoying Fife through . . . Crafts

For the past ten years or so there has been an increasing interest in the traditional skills which produce handcrafted goods, and Fife has a growing number of craft centres which are catering directly for the visitor. Fife pottery is much collected too, both the antique variety and the pots made today, and collectors continually search for the silver made by itinerant craftsmen before the Assay Act of 1836, particularly by the St Andrews silversmiths. Modern Fife provides a comfortable ambience and fine work environments in which craftsfolk can work, and the scope of their activities is increasing every year. Craft businesses from Tayport (jewellery) to Limekilns (local crafts) are providing more visitor facilities in the form of showrooms and demonstrations.

Here are a few places to visit which offer *craft skills demonstrations* and *product exhibitions.*

In the west of Fife there are:

Robert Murray, 6 Spruce Grove, Dunfermline, offering silver jewellery.

Ptarmigan Screencraft Ltd, 3 Knockhill Close, Lochgelly, where George Mackie offers art-slate.

The Tangles, 6 Main Street, Limekilns is run by Sheila Hutton and shows knitwear and local crafts.

In the Kirkcaldy area there are:

The multi-range craft workshops of Balbirnie Craft Centre, By Markinch, Glenrothes.

Eddergoll Studios, Balgonie Castle, By Markinch, where there is a leather carver's shop and that of tapestry weavers.

And in North East Fife there are:

Jim Allen's card cut-out models at 49, The Mount, Balmullo.

Anstruther Pottery, 1 Shore St, Anstruther.

Auchterlonies, 2 Golf Place, St Andrews, where golf clubs are made.

Church Square Ceramics, 4 Church Sq, St Andrews.

Crail Pottery, 75 Nethergate, Crail.

Designer Jewellery Workshop, Horsemarket St, Falkland.

Elspeth Barker, 2 King Street, Tayport, producing ear-rings and enamelled work.

Eileen Gardner, Bellfield, Priory Road, Gauldry, producing water colours.

David Joy, Glass Engraving, The Grange, St. Andrews.

Jenifer McWilliam, 12 High St, Auchtermuchty, bobbincraft.

Anne Lightwood Pottery and Porcelain, 55 South St, St Andrews.

Loft Workshop, Main Street, Upper Largo.

Pitlessie Woodcarver, 7 Crossgates, Pitlessie.

And many more promoted by the Fife Craft Association.

CHAPTER 1

Dunfermline and West Fife

I. North Queensferry–Inchgarvie–Inverkeithing–Dalgety Bay–Aberdour–Inchcolm–Inchkeith–Burntisland–Kinghorn

The medieval pilgrims had the best of it. Despite the whims of tide and wind they took a leisurely ferry passage over the Forth on their way to the shrines at Dunfermline Abbey and St Andrews Cathedral, and had time to stop and stare at the Kingdom of Fife as it loomed out of the morning mist. The landfall at North Queensferry has long been a place of spectacular views and bracing air – Sir James Simpson, the inventor of chloroform, often sent patients to recuperate. Today the traveller has the choice of crossing into Fife at North Queensferry by way of the road bridge inaugurated by Her Majesty the Queen Elizabeth II on 4 September 1964, or by the rail bridge officially opened by her great-grandfather on 4 March 1890 when he was HRH Albert Edward, Prince of Wales.

It was Margaret, Saxon wife of King Malcolm III, who first set the fashion of crossing the *watergang*, or passage, over the Firth of Forth. She regularly sailed aboard the royal ferry to and from her chapel at Edinburgh Castle. On her death at Edinburgh Castle in 1093, her remains were carried over the same route in solemn procession to her last resting place at Dunfermline.

According to the *Register of Dunfermline*, King David I granted to the Abbot and Convent of Dunfermline the 'passage and ship of Enderkeithin' in 1129; thus he it was who instituted a regular ferry service through his decree that all travellers should have free passage over the Forth water to the Court at Dunfermline. At first the passage was called *passagium de Inverkeithin*, but after the formal grant of lands it was named for all time *ad portum reginae* after the famous queen. The ferry rights were confirmed by subsequent monarchs, and popes, and Malcolm IV added the grant of hospital lands to the monks at Ferry Fields. These lands were undoubtedly those associated with the 'hospital' which Turgot, Bishop of St Andrews in the early 12th century, tells us was set up here by Queen Margaret for pilgrims and the poor.

When the ferrying of passengers became too much for the monks at Dunfermline, the franchise was given to 'substantial seamen'. Down the centuries the ferry feus were granted to various people on both sides of the Forth, but the ferry charges were continually in dispute, especially when ferrymen (and women) started to charge clerics. A fixed charge of one penny per person and twopence per horse was fixed by Act of Parliament in 1474. At the Reformation the governance of the ferry was given to the Lordship of Dunfermline and was bestowed on Anne of Denmark as a wedding gift by James VI in 1589.

In time the water passage was divided into sixteen shares and feued to various people who attempted to extract as large fares as possible from travellers. The smooth running of the services depended upon the weather and the mood of the ferryfolk, but in 1749 at the Court of Admiralty sitting at Dunfermline new regulations were laid down for the proper conduct of the ferries. A copy of the regulations was to be available for all to see at John Douglas's public house at North Ferry (likewise at William Hill's public house at South Queensferry). By the 18th century the ferry charge per person had risen to '1/6d Scots' and '4/– Scots' per horse, and a coach cost £1-10-0d.

In 1809 the ferry was vested not in private operators but in Trustees who now controlled the regulation of the ferries. New piers were constructed with shelters for passengers and crew; it is likely that up to the 16th century there had been no quays at all, with boats beaching at Haughend. A steamboat, designed to suit the new piers, was put into service on 1 October 1821 and was named *Queen Margaret;* she began a long line of ferryboats which ended with the celebrated *Mary Queen of Scots* (1949) and the *Sir William Wallace* (1955).

Trustees adminstered the ferry services until 1867 when the rights were purchased by the North British Railway Co; the company operated the ferry until 1893 when it was taken over by successive towage companies until in 1926 the railway company resumed control. In 1934 the firm of William Denny

Ferry routes from South Queensferry to Fife's southern shore at North Queensferry were plied from the 12th century to the opening of the new road bridge – seen under construction to the left of the picture – in 1964. The steam ferry *Sir William Wallace* sits at the quay dominated by the Forth Railway Bridge, built 1883-90 *(D.C. Thomson & Co Ltd).*

& Bros Ltd took over the running of the ferries and brought into service the diesel-electric paddle-driven boat the *Queen Margaret,* and the first all-welded Scottish ferry *Robert the Bruce.* The ferry ceased at the opening of the new road bridge in 1964, but the old piers can still be seen on the shoreline in their latest rôle as shelter for pleasure craft.

There is a retained cosiness about North Queensferry as it nestles under the Ferry Hills, which once the Jews wished to purchase from Alexander III as their refuge. North Queensferry was formerly a tight-knit community where only locals were allowed to act as boatmen and publicans; today it is a more cosmopolitan place with residents seeking employment elsewhere. Right in the heart of North Queensferry is the ancient chapel and burying ground. The chapel grounds once took in the roadways outside the present site, and the high walls around the pre-Reformation chapel were built by local sailors in 1752. In the 17th-century graveyard this epitaph spells out the former way of life:

> Now here we lay at anchor
> With many of our fleet,
> In hopes to weigh at the last day
> Our Admiral Christ to meet.

The west wall of the burial ground is formed partly by the gable of the chapel founded by Robert I, the Bruce, in the early 14th century and tended by the monks of Dunfermline Abbey. The church is dedicated to Our Lord's cousin, St James the Apostle, who was fittingly the patron saint of pilgrims. The chapel was extensively damaged by Cromwell's men in 1651.

From the chapel, which is a location on the North Queensferry Heritage Trail, it is a short walk up The Brae (Ferryhills Road) to two interesting sites. The Jubilee Well (1899) abuts the site of the village waterhouse erected around 1783 to regulate the water supply; across the road is the Old School House built by subscription in 1827 and used until 1876.

The houses at North Queensferry climb boldly up the Ferry Hills which were long hewn for their fine stone; stone from these cliffs went to pave the streets of London and was shipped to Russia to build the fortifications of the Baltic port of Kronshlot on the Isle of Kotlin. The MOD Signal Station sits on Battery Hill at the edge of an old quarry face above the Wee Sea and the hill takes its name from the time when cannon were placed here as a precaution in the Napoleonic Wars.

In mid-channel the mighty three-cantilever railway bridge uses the island of Inchgarvie as a stepping stone. The now deserted island, with its old ruined forts, was once an important strategic location. It was mentioned early in Scotland's history, for here in the 8th century, Angus, the Pictish High King, displayed the head of the leader of the invading Angles set upon a pole as a dreadful warning to other potential adversaries. The island was granted to the Dundas family by James IV in 1491 and permission was agreed to raise a castle to guard against the 'English rovers and pirates of

The 'Hat and Ribbon Race' parade, led by the Burgh Officer with beribboned hat balanced on a halberd, processes down the High Street, Inverkeithing. The race takes place each year at the opening of the Lammas Market, which was revived in 1964, and began as an event for herdsmen with the prize of a hat with ribbons for the winning herdsman's 'lass' *(The Dunfermline Press)*.

other nations'. Down the centuries the fort was used as an isolation place for victims of infectious diseases and as a state prison, but it fell into neglect in the 16th century. The island was regarrisoned in Cromwell's day but was rendered useless in 1651 to keep it out of Old Noll's hands. Again in 1799 Inchgarvie was refortified, this time to repel the privateer John Paul Jones. The Dundas family sold the island to the early railway entrepreneurs and it became more celebrated as a workplace for the gangs fabricating the Forth Railway Bridge. The Royal Garrison Artillery manned the island in World War 1 and Inchgarvie gave its name to the sprats caught in neighbouring waters, the 'garvies'.

The Forth Rail Bridge, begun in January 1883 and completed in March 1890, was designed by Sir John Fowler and Sir Benjamin Baker, the contractors being Messrs

Tancred, Arrol & Co Ltd. Some 5000 men laboured on the bridge and the cost of construction was £3,000,000. A continuous structure, nearly 1⅝ miles long, the Forth Railway Bridge with its distinctive cantilever structures has a permanent staff of 20 painters using 17 tons of paint annually to keep it in good trim in a four-year cycle. Its neighbour the Forth Road Bridge is of the same length and Treasury authority was given in 1958 for its £20,000,000 cost and the bridge was opened in 1964. Although not of pioneer design like the railway bridge, it has a distinctive bowed effect, the work of Giles Gilbert Scott & Partners.

North Queensferry can be reached from the A/M90 via the B980 and B981 from Rosyth, and from the shore the steep old coach road can be taken over the Ferry Hills via Carlingnose. To the right is Port Laing and Cruickness and the site of a lazaretto, dating from the Middle Ages when the scourge of society was leprosy. The road leads through the old hamlet of Jamestown, where magnesia was once worked and salt panned, to the Inner Bay of Inverkeithing.

On the western outskirts of Inverkeithing the shipbreaking yard of Messrs James A. White & Co Ltd flanks Cruickness Road; this firm succeeded that of Thomas W. Ward Ltd (1921) in 1981. Their neighbours across the bay are Caldwell's Paper Mill (1893) which were incorporated into the GP Inveresk Group in 1981. Hope Street leads into the heart of what was medieval Inverkeithing at High Street and Church Street. Situated astride the old north-south route and affording safe anchorage in its eponymous bay, Inverkeithing has a charter granted by William I, the Lion, around 1165. Some say its shores sheltered the vessels of Agricola, but certainly there seems to have been a settlement here since long before William's charter. In the 12th century Inverkeithing belonged to Gospatrick, Earl of Dunbar, but in time the land passed into the hands of the Moubrays of Barnbougle who held sway until the 17th century. Documents show that David I was a landowner here and he set the fashion for Inverkeithing as a medieval watering place. Robert III's wife, Annabella Drummond, resided at Rotmills Inns in the town and died here in 1403. So important was the town that the Convention of Royal Burghs was held here in 1487.

Oil products are an important part of Fife's modern commercial scene and NGL carrier *Isocardia* is seen being loaded at Braefoot Bay Marine Terminal which is situated between Aberdour and Dalgety Bay. The products are piped 4½ miles from the Fife NGL Plant at Mossmoran by the world's longest underground refrigerated pipeline *(Shell UK Exploration and Production).*

Inverkeithing once had a considerable coastal trade and coal was shipped in large quantities from the nearby St Davids harbour, from the mines owned by Sir John Henderson of Fordell. A horse railway between Halbeath and Inverkeithing opened in 1783 for the transportation of coal and this wagon road lasted until 1867. The piers at Inverkeithing were lengthened, strengthened and repaired at various times for the ships which plied between the Forth and Russia, Germany and France. The prosperity of the 18th and 19th centuries was built on hundreds of years of trading, for in 1270, for instance, Lombardic merchants established trading rights at Inverkeithing.

Modern Inverkeithing sports a number of important ancient buildings. In Church Street stands the Parish Church of St

Peter, which started as a wooden Celtic church and was developed into a Norman stone structure bequeathed to Dunfermline Abbey in 1139. All that remains of the pre-Reformation church is the 15th-century tower, for the church was destroyed by fire in 1825; it was restored in 1900. One treasure of the church is the font discovered during excavations in 1807; it was probably concealed from the despoilers at the Reformation and is thought to have been gifted by Annabella Drummond and Robert III at the baptism of their son, David, Duke of Rothesay.

Opposite St Peter's is the distinctive, turreted L-shaped town house known as Fordell's Lodgings, built 1666-71 by Sir John Henderson of Fordell. Providence House of 1688 – so called because its lintel is carved with 'God's Providence is my Inheritance' – is worthy of notice too. Rosebery House in King Street belonged to the Rosebery family and is a much-altered 16th-century edifice. The house was once known as 'The Toofall' before it was purchased by the Earl of Rosebery and was owned by John, Earl of Dunbar in 1668; in 1672 the house was gifted by Charles II to the 3rd Earl of Lauderdale. In the High Street is the house where one of Inverkeithing's famous sons was born in 1735: Sir Samuel Greig, the son of a shipowning baillie of the royal burgh, who became a distinguished Admiral in the Imperial Russian Navy. In Heriot Street stands Moffat Cottage named after the famous Scottish divine and missionary James Moffat who explored the Cape and translated the Bible into modern English. Another celebrated missionary, David Livingstone, is associated with the dwelling too; Livingstone married Moffat's daughter and was a frequent visitor to Inverkeithing; at the rear of the cottage is the summerhouse built by Livingstone during his stays.

The Hospitium of Greyfriars Monastery stands in Queen Street and was possibly founded as early as the 13th century by Philip de Moubray, Lord of Barnbougle, and was used by friars of the Order of St Francis. The friary was restored in 1935 and now houses the Burgh Museum. Inverkeithing's Town House with its pepperpot steeple replaced an older Tolbooth in 1770. Fife's tolbooths incidentally were the equivalent of the English town hall and were the burgh tax offices and administrative centres; here too would be sited a prison. The town bell, now in

Reached by ferry from Aberdour, during June to mid-September, the 12th-century Augustinian priory of Inchcolm was founded by King Alexander I, and is an unexpected bonus for visitors to Fife. Its old fortifications now garrisoned by seabirds, the island offers fine walks to explore a hermit's cell, a Viking grave, an ammunition tunnel and a bird sanctuary *(D.C. Thomson & Co Ltd).*

the museum, was made in 1667 by the craftsman Johannes Burgherhuys of Zeeland. Above the door of the Town House is the old burgh's coat of arms; it shows St Peter the 1st-century Apostle and Martyr with tiara, key and a church on the dexter side of the arms, with a ship on the sinister side. Within the Town House are the Council Chamber and the Burgh Court room, which were used up to May 1975.

Inverkeithing's Mercat Cross has had a number of sites. Originally it stood at the north end of High Street and was moved to face the Town House in 1799 as it was impeding the passage of stagecoaches; today it is located in Bank Street a few yards round the corner. In medieval times the mercat cross was the centre of a Scottish community. At the cross important proclamations were read, 'tidings of weal and woe' as the old chroniclers had it, and merchants gathered on market days to display their wares. The mercat crosses were places of punishment too where the guilty were accused and maybe flogged. In some burghs the *jougs* (a hinged collar fastened to the stonework through which the offender's neck was placed) would hang at the cross. Some poor souls were arrainged and burned for witchcraft at the mercat cross too. Historians see the mercat cross as developing from the old standing stones of prehistoric times, for in tribal times certain stones were set apart for oaths and rituals as a centrepiece of the old tribal areas. The mercat cross at Inverkeithing is one of the finest remaining in Scotland. It is surmounted by the Unicorn of Scotland and dates from 1398. Two of its shields bear the arms of Scotland and the other two the arms of Annabella Drummond and the Douglas family. Sundials have been ingeniously worked into intersecting octagonal prisms. The cross was possibly set up as a memorial of the marriage of the Duke of Rothesay with the daughter of the Earl of Douglas. The unicorn was added in 1688 and is the work of John Boyd, mason of South Queensferry. At the base of the cross is a plaque commemorating the Battle of Inverkeithing, 20 July 1651, in which Cromwell's army vanquished the Scots.

In common with most Scottish burghs Inverkeithing had four main fairs, at Candlemass (February), Beltane (May), Lammas (August), and Martinmas (November) – from the latter we get our word 'mart'. Today the Lammas Fair remains and the fair was described in the burgh records of 1652 as a day of 'fun, frolic, fit races, ale and drunken folks'; it drew people from miles around and James IV bought his horses at Inverkeithing's Lammas Fair. The annual 'Hat and Ribbon' Race takes place at the Lammas Fair at Inverkeithing and dates back to the 17th century; it is run on the Friday evening of the fair. The race is preceded by a procession led by a pipe band, the district officer who holds aloft a top hat decorated with ribbons, and a group of local and district representatives. The Inverkeithing Highland Games are also held at the Lammas weekend.

The B981 passes through Inverkeithing and links with the A92 to Kirkcaldy. The hamlet of Hillend lies at the foot of Letham Hill Wood. To the right down the B916 is Fordell Castle, which stands in a magnificent wooded parkland on the edge of a ravine above the Keithing Burn. Based on a 13th-century estate gifted to the monks of Inchcolm by Richard de

Rossend Castle towers above the docks at Burntisland. Once called Burntisland Castle, some portions date from the 16th century and the old keep probably replaces a 14th-century structure belonging to Dunfermline Abbey. Mary, Queen of Scots visited the castle in 1563, as did Cromwell in 1651. For decades local politicians wished to demolish the castle, but it has been renovated in recent times in one of Fife's most exciting redevelopments and is now privately owned offices *(Fife Regional Council).*

Camera around 1220, Fordell Castle was the seat of the Henderson family wholly from the 16th century to the 20th century; they consolidated the estate and invested heavily in mining operations. Across the estate once ran Scotland's first private railway to transport coal to St Davids harbour. Fordell estate also sponsored salt panning, and with coal and salt interests the family were consequently the major employers in the area. These were the days when the miners were virtual slaves, to be bought and sold with the equipment of the collieries. Sir John Henderson, sometime MP for Fife, Dysart, Kirkcaldy Burghs and Stirling Burghs, granted the miners of Fordell and Dalgety their freedom and for many decades this grant was celebrated in the Fordell Annual Parade.

Fordell Castle today is a late 16th-century fortalice of the Z-plan; that is, it is a version of the building design of two wings set at diagonally opposite corners of a main block allowing all-round flanking fire in time of siege. The castle was long maintained as a folly by the Henderson descendants after Sir John Henderson built a more modern mansion in 1721. Today the castle is the home of Nicholas Fairbairn, Member of Parliament for Perth and Kinross constituency. He bought the property from a relative-in-law of Lord Attlee and set about making the place habitable and has spent much time recreating the Caroline garden which was long deemed a masterpiece.

The Scottish Scouts Association National Camping and Training Centre is situated at Fordell Firs a mile north of Hillend village.

From Hillend the A92 leads on to the industrial estate of Donibristle set on the site of the wartime Royal Navy Air Service Station. A new road system branches right just before the industrial estate and leads down to Dalgety Bay. The land hereabouts was once part of the estates of the Hendersons of Fordell, the Moubrays of Cockairnie and the Earl of Moray.

Dalgety has developed from a 19th-century village into a new town. Construction began in the early 1960s and the location was to see Scotland's first privately-built new town. Tradition has it that the village dates back to the 14th century and that Dalgety's first inhabitants came from Denmark, victims of religious persecution. Once Dalgety's superior coal (again a part of the Fordell mining enterprises) was a must for the steam navigation companies. Despite Admiral Sir Philip Calderwood Durham of Fordell's investment of £2000 in a new harbour for Dalgety the coal trade declined (as did the demand for local salt) and the village entered a new low; buildings were demolished and people scattered; the hamlet that once supported St Davids harbour became a lost village too. Now most of the residents of Dalgety commute to Edinburgh and their 'executive type' dwellings are far removed from the old bothies.

The historical star attraction at Dalgety is St Bridget's Church, reached from the A92, passing Old Dalgety Parish Church down the narrow Four Lums Road. Built by the monks of Inchcolm, the old church of St Bridget is made up of a later

'To the illustrious Alexander III the last of Scotland's Celtic Kings who was accidentally killed near this spot. March XIX MCCLXXXVI erected on the Sex-Centenary of his death.' Thus reads the inscription for the 1886 Peterhead granite memorial to King Alexander III, on the A921 east of Kinghorn, above Pettycur Bay Sands. The horror of the king's death was summed up by the Augustinian Canon Andrew Wyntoun (c.1355-1422) in his *Chronicle:* 'Quen Alysandyr oure kyng was dede, that Scotland led in luive and le, away wes sonce of ale and brede, of wyne and wax, of gamyn and gle; oure gold wes changed into lede. Cryst! Born into virgynyte, succour Scotland and remede, that stad is in perplexyte.'

two-storey building comprising a burial vault on the ground floor and a 'laird's loft' above, from which access was gained to a western gallery within the church. The edifice was dedicated to the Ulster-born 5th-century saint the Abbess Bridget in 1244. St Bridget's was used as a residence by the Covenanting pastor Andrew Donaldson who was ejected at the restoration of Episcopacy in 1661. Just outside the walls is a small stone building which acted as a watch-house against the Resurrectionists (body-snatchers), whose activities kept the anatomy tables of Edinburgh well filled. The church was de-roofed in 1830.

The estate of Donibristle stretched from St Davids harbour to Aberdour and was the seat of the Earl of Moray. The lands once belonged to the monks of Inchcolm, and the first castle on the site belonged to James Stewart, Lord of Doune, Commendator of Inchcolm; it became the principal residence of his son who entered immortality as 'the Bonnie Earl of Moray' famed in ballad:

> Ye Highlands and ye Lowlands,
> O where hae ye been?
> They ha'e slain the Earl of Moray
> And laid him on the green.

The 'green' was the shoreline in front of Donibristle House, and there on 7 February 1592 the Bonnie Earl, the darling of the Protestant cause, was murdered by the Earl of Huntly, leader of the Roman Catholic party. The Bonnie Earl had earned the jealousy of King James VI, for the balladmongers linked the handsome Moray with his queen, Anne of Denmark: . . .

> He was a braw gallant,
> And he played at the gluve,
> And the bonnie Earl of Moray,
> Oh, he was the Queen's luve.

That, along with the Bonnie Earl's association with the king's enemies, was enough to sign his death warrant. After the murder Huntly caused Donibristle House to be burned to the ground and although it was replaced, it burned down again in 1858. The Moray estates were sold to the property developers who built the new town of Dalgety Bay in the 1960s.

The name Donibristle is remembered too in these parts because of the terrible mining disaster at Donibristle colliery – sited a few miles to the north of Dalgety near to the A907 Dunfermline/Kirkcaldy road, east of Crossgates – on Monday, 26 August 1901, when eight miners perished. Many poems and

Dunfermline's original Celtic church was replaced by the abbey dedicated to the Holy Trinity by King Malcolm III and Queen Margaret in 1072. Today the east end of the medieval abbey church forms the town's parish church, rebuilt 1818-21. The west end of the abbey church is retained as an ancient monument. Located close by the east gable of the modern church are the remains of the Shrine of St Margaret, Malcolm's queen who was canonised in 1250.

songs were written about the underground tragedy; this excerpt of one recalls the grief:

> Between Donibristle and Cowdenbeath,
> Moss Morran's desolate plain does lie,
> And here the poor miners met their death
> Beneath an autumn's dismal sky.

At Mossmorran today the oil-giants Shell and Esso have two plants where natural gas from the Brent oilfield in the North Sea is processed for export to world markets. Finally the products are piped four miles south to the tanker terminal at Braefoot Bay, near Aberdour, to be shipped worldwide.

The A92 leads on to the still comparatively peaceful old town of Aberdour, a holiday place which can offer landscapes and seascapes in equally rich measure. Modern Aberdour is made up of Easter Aberdour, which was made into a Burgh of

Regality in 1638, and Wester Aberdour which was a Burgh of Barony from 1501. These two ancient burghs – the word originally meant a fortified place – are good examples of the old Scots burgh system. There were two main types of burgh in Scotland – Royal Burghs, and Burghs of Regality and Barony. The first showed that a town belonged to the king, while the others indicated that the superior was a cleric or of the influential laity. As a Burgh of Regality Easter Aberdour owed title to the Earls of Morton, while its Western counterpart was a Barony under the Abbey of Inchcolm and the Moray family.

The town has seen a great deal of expansion since World War II, but still sports some fine 18th-century buildings and 19th-century houses. Among the showpieces of Aberdour is its church, a gem of Scottish ecclesiastical architecture. St Fillan's church stands by the road leading to the Silver Sands beach and dates from the 12th century; it was used continuously for worship until 1796. It was derelict until 1925 when it was restored and rededicated. Today it is a church of many phases of architecture, from its 15th-century entrance porch to its Norman windows. Tradition has it that Robert I, the Bruce, and thought to be a leper, worshipped at the now-sealed leper's squint at Aberdour after the battle of Bannockburn in 1314.

Nearby is the castle of Aberdour, the oldest part of which is the rhomboidal tower of the 14th century; the other buildings were added during the 16th-17th centuries. In the grounds a fine dovecote or doocot remains in good repair. The castle became the home of the Regent Morton who became the 4th Earl of that name in 1553. The Mortons took over the castle from the Mortimers who inherited it from the Norman barons, the Viponts, and held the castle until the middle of the 18th century; the last occupant was Robert Watson of Muirhouse who died there in 1791. Thereafter the castle fell into disrepair.

Aberdour, once called the 'Fife Riviera', has a flourishing natural history. From its shores numerous seabirds and waders may be observed. The area is well wooded too, with fine species of Spanish chestnut and walnut trees; the woods around sport fine displays of yellow iris, marsh marigolds and *doronicum* (leopard's bane).

During the spring and summer months a ferry plies between Aberdour's West Sands and the island of Inchcolm which lies about a mile and a half west of the town across the curiously named Mortimer's Deep. Local tradition has it that the cadaver of the unpopular landlord of the island, Sir Alan de Mortimer, was being ferried to Inchcolm for burial by the monks when they 'lost' it overboard.

In the year 1123, wrote Walter Bower, abbot of Inchcolm, in the *Scotichronicon*, King Alexander I was driven upon the rocks at Inchcolm during a storm; to give thanks for his deliverance he founded a priory for monks of the Augustinian order who would give care and prayers for shipwrecked mariners; the convent was erected into an abbey in 1235.

The island of Inchcolm is about a mile and a half long and consists of two hill areas reaching 90ft above the sea and connected by a narrow isthmus sometimes mantled with a veil of water. It has been known at different times as the 'Iona of the East', 'St Colme's Inch', and perhaps most romantically as Aemonia. Today, as well as the custodian of the abbey, Inchcolm is the home of a wide range of seabirds and delightful varieties of flowers in nooks and crannies. The monastic site itself is situated in the hollow of the two hills and overlooks the Forth on two sides. An abbey of great wealth in the Middle Ages, it has a range of 13th and 14th-century architecture worthy of note. Near the church is a primitive hermit's oratory – the one in which King Alexander and his suite are thought to have sheltered for three days of storms – of around the 9th century, bearing witness to the island's thousand years of sanctity; here too it is said St Columba, the 6th-century Abbot and Confessor of Iona, stayed while converting the Picts to Christianity. Standing two stories high, the abbey still retains its belfry and dove holes, cloisters and vaulted Norman nave, and its treasured frescoes showing a funeral procession of clerics.

The abbey was pillaged many times, and after the disastrous battle of Pinkie in 1547, when the English defeated the Scots army, it became a fort and subsequently a state prison and pirates' nest before it was acquired by Sir James Stewart in 1581. Inchcolm was then left to decay in peace until it was fortified during the Napoleonic War. In 1845 when the

Russian fleet of Czar Nicholas I arrived in the Forth the island was used as a hospital.

There have been many burials at Inchcolm including bishops of Dunkeld, but none were more famous than the followers of Sueno, vanquished King of Norway. Shakespeare recalled the event in *Macbeth*.

> Sueno, the Norway's King, craves composition;
> Nor would we deign him burial of his men
> Till he disbursed, at Saint Colme's Inch,
> Ten thousand dollars to our general use.

Inchcolm's neighbours in the Forth are the Cow and Calves and Inchmickery, all in Lothian Region; but to the east and in Fife Region is the island of Inchkeith once called *L'île des chevaux* (Island of Horses) by the French troops garrisoned there in the mid-1500s. Almost a mile long and rising to 180 ft, Inchkeith was granted to Robert de Keith in 1010 by Malcolm II in return for assistance in battle against the Danes.

A curious tale is remembered from James IV's reign, for he is supposed to have carried out the strange experiment of placing on the island a deaf and dumb woman and two babies. His objective was to see what language the children would grow to speak – the outcome of the experiment is not known, but one chronicler fancifully averred that the children spoke Hebrew! The king put the island to a more practical use too as a training ground for his hawks. In the 15th century Inchkeith was used as a refuge for plague victims and in James V's reign it was granted to Sir Alexander Wood of Largo on the forfeiture of John, Lord Glamis. There followed the days of the 'Rough Wooing' – Henry VIII of England's attempt to have the infant Mary Queen of Scots as a bride for his son Edward – and Inchkeith developed as a military base and remained so until after World War II. By way of several owners, from the Strathmores of Glamis to the Campbells of Argyll, Inchkeith passed to the Dukes of Buccleuch who sold it to the government in 1878. The first lighthouse was built on the island in 1803 on the site of one of the medieval forts; a holophotal dioptric lens was fitted in 1889. Today Inchkeith has an automatic light and is privately owned.

The west end of Dunfermline Abbey leads the eye to the central tower of 1818-21 which displays the lettering of the name of Robert I, the Bruce (1274-1329), Scotland's national hero. The remains of the Royal palace – where King Charles I was born in 1600 – are in the foreground, with the west elevation of the monks' refectory rising above and next to the gatehouse astride the pend of Monastery Street.

From Aberdour the A82 leads directly to Burntisland; just before dropping down into the town the road passes very close to the curious 'castle' at Easterheughs – this was built 1946-59 by William Thomas, a retired works manager. He based his plans on 17th-century Scottish architectural styles and used stone from the demolished Otterstone House. At the foot of Aberdour Road lies the complex of BA Aluminium Co Ltd which began as a commercial enterprise in 1917. The aluminium works and the Burntisland Shipbuilding Co were once the burgh's main employers. Founded by the Ayre brothers in 1918, the Burntisland Shipbuilding Co lasted through the Depression but in the 1960s it ran into financial difficulties and the company went into voluntary liquidation in 1968. Once the docks at Burntisland hummed with coal exports and bauxite imports. James V used the town as a naval base and the town saw the first railway ferry in the world open in 1850 between Burntisland and Granton. The ferries ceased in 1952. Burntisland once had its own brewery too, that of the Grange Distillery belonging to William Young & Co which had been established in 1786. The Youngs were benefactors of the town and produced a celebrated Lowland malt 'OB Whisky'; the firm ceased in 1916.

The verifiable history of Burntisland begins in the 12th century when the harbour and lands around belonged to Dunfermline Abbey. The abbey built the original Burntisland Castle (Rossend Castle), it is said in 1119, and the old church of the Kirkton; so, round these two sites the town evolved. Burntisland was chartered in 1541 and in 1586 it was proclaimed a royal burgh with John Clephane as its first Provost. Cromwell captured the burgh in 1651 and Samuel Pepys noted that Burntisland was bombarded by the Dutch in 1667.

In medieval times Burntisland had two weekly markets and a 'common fair' dedicated conjointly to the Apostles SS Peter and Paul. Once too, the town conducted a colourful ceremony of 'Crowning the Queen of the Fair' at the Big Knowe; the ceremonies fell into disuse but have been revived in the form of a 'Summer Queen', who is still crowned on the Links. Burntisland's present Fair began, tradition has it, as a horse race between cavalrymen from Cromwell's Army in 1654. Burntislands Highland Games are still held in mid-July.

The little church of Burntisland at Kirkton was re-dedicated to St Serf by Bishop de Bernham in 1243 and was sited in modern Church Street. The predominating church today, however, is St Columba's, which boasts of being the first church built after the Reformation, 1592-95. It retains many interesting features including the panels of the mariner's loft and the signs of the various long defunct trade guilds; the church contains an unusual canopied pew built for Sir Robert Melville – latterly it was known as the 'Magistrates' Pew' and was used for 'The Kirkin' o' the Coonsel'; this being a ceremony in which the local Town Council (which ceased at Burntisland in 1975) processed gowned to the church for a civic service. At a meeting at Burntisland in 1601 the General Assembly proposed the Authorised version of the Bible.

It was not often in history that a Scotswoman defied social convention. One such was Mary Somerville, the daughter of

Vice-Admiral Sir William Fairfax, one of Nelson's captains. Born at Jedburgh in 1780, and brought up at Burntisland, she struggled all her life for her own education – 'Latin's no for lassies', her Burntisland dominie had told her – and for the education of women in general. She went on to become a distinguished mathematician and her fame is remembered in the Oxford College of 1879 which bears her name. The house where she lived in the now renamed Somerville Square is an inspired renovation of old and new; in fact the square is worthy of study as an example of how a formerly dingy row of 17th and 19th-century houses can form an essential part of urban renewal. The painted ceilings which were once in the house are now preserved in Edinburgh Castle where they were moved in 1957.

Overlooking Burntisland harbour, the Rossend Castle we see today began as an L-shaped tower-house and was constructed around 1554. The tower was extended in the early 17th century and again in the 19th to provide additional accommodation at its lower levels. This replaced an earlier structure possibly of the 12th century built by the clergy of Dunfermline Abbey. Certainly it was still in the ownership of the Abbot of Dunfermline, one George Durie, in the early 16th century, and was later confirmed by Mary Queen of Scots for Sir Robert Melville. No comment on Rossend Castle would be complete without a mention of the castle's most romantic interlude – even though the castle was held by Rob Roy McGregor for James VIII & III the Old Pretender.

In 1563 Mary Queen of Scots was en route for St Andrews when she stayed over at Rossend Castle; an uninvited member of her train was the handsome and hopelessly romantic French poet Pierre de Chastelard. The poet was greatly enamoured of the queen and he had already secreted himself in her bedchamber at Holyrood Palace; Chastelard had been discovered, admonished and expelled, the queen having absolved him of the capital charge of *lèse majesté* . At Rossend, Chastelard was again discovered in her privy chamber and for this indiscretion Mary ordered him to be slain. Chastelard was taken to St Andrews and executed at the mercat cross. Just before he died he is said to have shouted: 'Adieu, thou most beautiful and most cruel Princess in the world'.

Rossend Castle continued to be owned by the Melville family for many years, but in the 18th century it passed to the Campbells and then to the Wemyss family. In the 1930s it was taken over by Burntisland Town Council; steadily it fell into disrepair and was severely vandalised. Plans to demolish it were stoutly resisted by interested parties and eventually the building was restored by a firm of architects to be used as offices; this is the rôle of the castle today.

The A92 takes a sharp turn left at Burntisland and follows the Links, once the town's golf course on lands ceded by James V in exchange for harbouring rights, and the railway to continue past the Kingswood Hotel – erstwhile home of the Johnson family, sugar traders in Jamaica – to the headland of Pettycur, formerly the northern terminal of a Forth Ferry. There are still milestones in Fife which bear the name Pettycur, relics of when travellers might calculate their distance from the ferry; the main coach route went from Pettycur to Woodhaven on the Tay, via Cupar.

To the north of Pettycur stands Witch Hill, the place where the witches were executed. Nearby Grange was the home of William Kirkcaldy of Grange who was implicated in the assassination of Cardinal David Beaton at St Andrews in 1546 and who later languished in the French fortress of Mont St Michel for his pains. William Kirkcaldy was a noted soldier and he was hanged in 1573 for his opposition to the Regent Morton. A farmhouse now incorporates all that remains of Kirkcaldy's 16th-century home.

Halfway to Kinghorn stands the Celtic Cross in memory of Alexander III, the last of Scotland's Celtic Kings and victor over King Haakon IV of Norway at the Battle of Largs in 1263. On 19 March 1286 Alexander attended a council at Edinburgh. It was a dark and stormy night as he rode into Burntisland, but the king would press on as he was anxious to join his wife at the Tower of Kinghorn. In the dark he became separated from his aides, and on the precipice of Kinghorn Ness his horse stumbled and Alexander was thrown over the cliffs. The memorial of Peterhead granite was set up in 1886 to mark this event whose consequence plunged Scotland into a protracted period of calamity.

A popular place with tourists and caravanners, Kinghorn was

The old-style stooks, the waste bing and pit near Kelty, in this picture of September 1948, recall the mixture of mining and farming in Fife's former commercial heritage. Now pit bings and collieries have been landscaped into leisure areas like the imaginative Lochore Meadows Country Park to the east of Kelty on the B920 from Lochgelly *(D.C. Thomson & Co Ltd).*

once a prosperous spinning and shipbuilding centre, described once as a 'douce, well-aired town'. It was an ancient settlement when David I created it a royal burgh in the 12th century. Kinghorn Castle, once Glamis Tower because of its ownership by the Lyons of Glamis, has now vanished but it was once a favourite haven for both monarchs and nobility alike. In the old regal hierarchy of Scotland the name of Kinghorn appears for the offices of Constable of Kinghorn and Keeper of the King's Door which were important court positions. Today too, the town's name appears in a Scottish earldom, that of Strathmore and Kinghorne.

Before Kinghorn received its Townhouse in 1822 the site was occupied by a medieval edifice, St Leonard's Tower, once a chapel which fell to secular use. The parish church stands by the sea, down the Nethergate, and is on the site of several churches from Saxon times. The present one was rebuilt in 1894 and internally reconstructed in 1930; outside is the ruined choir of an earlier church. In medieval times Kinghorn had a hospital for the poor which was founded around 1478; this was set in the grounds of a chapel dedicated to St. James.

Several estates to the north of Kinghorn have featured prominently in Fife history. For instance Abden was once the land of the Bishops of St Andrews. The Castle of Pitteadie once belonged to the Earl of Rosslyn and is interesting for its gunports and two wings bearing the initials of Sir Henry Wardlaw (d.1631), chamberlain to James VI's queen, Anne of Denmark. The demolished Balmutto House was the seat of the Boswell family for five hundred years; it was built around a 15th-century keep with walls six feet thick. Seafield Tower lies in ruin by the sea, across the railway from the A92. It was the powerbase of the Moutray family from the 16th century. Kinghorn Loch lies to the northeast along the B923.

From Kinghorn the A92 leads straight to Kirkcaldy. If a round trip is contemplated from the Forth Road Bridge, to take in these Forth burghs, then a return by the A907 may be considered; it passes the much-ruined Knockdavie Castle (near Stenhouse Farm), once the seat of the Douglases. This progresses to the A92 just east of Dalgety Bay via the A987 and Cullaloe Reservoir with its range of waterbirds from great crested and little grebes to mute swans. Alternatively the A909 may be taken at Bernard's Smithy to rejoin the A907 for Dunfermline.

II. The auld grey toun – Dunfermline

More than a thousand years ago a handful of monks sought rest in what is now Pittencrieff Glen. They were priests of the Culdee Church, who had taken their name from *céli dé* , 'companions of God', and were a class of reformed clergy who are recorded as being in existence in the first half of the 9th century. They liked the place and founded a little church in the glen which was to give modern Dunfermline its name, which signifies 'the hill by the winding stream'. On this peninsulated hill, at Pittencrieff, King Malcolm III, bynamed Canmore, built a fortress tower around 1065, probably on the site of a Pictish habitation. It is probable too that this tower was the centre of the habitation of which the anonymous balladeer writes in *Sir Patrick Spens*:

> The king sits in Dumfermline town
> Drinking the blude-red wine.

Malcolm's patronage brought much needed work and succour to the starved and ragged people in the hamlet of wattle huts that had sprung up near to the chapel of the Culdees.

When Malcolm, son of King Duncan who was murdered by Macbeth, moved his court here from Forteviot in Perthshire, he set in motion a series of events which were to make Dunfermline an important Scottish capital; a rôle it kept until after the assassination of James I at Perth in 1437. To Malcolm's castle, the remains of which can still be seen in Pittencrieff Park, there came the Saxon Princess Margaret Atheling, granddaughter of Edmund Ironside. In 1069 she married Malcolm as his second wife and she began a further series of events, cultural and ecclesiastical, in her own right that were to transform Malcolm's old Celtic kingdom into a new Anglo-Norman realm.

Soon after her marriage, Queen Margaret, who had been educated by the Benedictines, persuaded Malcolm to enlarge the little Culdee chapel into a fine church for Benedictine monks. Dedicated to the Holy Trinity, the new church was formed, around 1072, into the priory peopled by Benedictines sent at Margaret's request by Lanfranc, Archbishop of Canterbury.

Queen Margaret died at Edinburgh Castle on 16 November 1093 on hearing of Malcolm's assassination. Her body was brought to Dunfermline for burial. Two of Margaret's sons, succeeding monarchs, carried on her work. In 1128 David I had the priory elevated into the abbey of Christ Church, with Prior Geoffrey as its first abbot.

In 1250 there happened an event that was to make Dunfermline famous throughout Christendom; Queen Margaret was canonised and her body was translated to a sumptuous shrine decorated with gold and precious stones.

The cult of St Margaret grew – her oratory, which was a cave in the side of Pittencrieff Glen, was a part of the itinerary of places to be visited by pilgrims, as was St Margaret's Well (now Headwell) and St Margaret's Hope, a sheltered bay on the Forth where she first landed in Scotland, and St Margaret's Stone between Rosyth and Dunfermline (near the gates of Pitreavie Castle) where she is supposed to have rested on her peregrinations through West Fife.

The abbey was to have five main periods of development: during 1128-1450 Margaret's church grew and its fine nave was laid out *circa* 1140; around 1240 the choir of the monastic church was extended and the shrine was built; considerable rebuilding took place in 1329, and in 1450 the west gable was rebuilt by Abbot Richard de Bothwell; and from 1594-99 the north-west tower of the nave was reconstructed by William Shaw. During the 17th century buttresses were erected to support the walls of the nave. And inside the splendour was continually enriched as seven kings, four queens, two princesses and five princes were laid to rest.

Slowly the abbey grew in power and wealth. Some twenty-six altars were endowed by individuals and guilds of the burgh. The Abbot of Dunfermline – who was a mitred abbot, making him second only to a diocesan bishop – ruled lands from Urquhart in Moray to within sight of the English border – he was overlord of four burghs and administered three Courts of Regality.

In Dunfermline's Maygate stands the Abbot's House, but this was not the home of a true abbot. The house was built after the Reformation in the late 16th century and is a fortalice in style which became the mansion of Robert Pitcairn, Commendator and titular Abbot of Dunfermline to 1584. Above the lintel of the house is the couplet:

SEN WORD IS THRALL AND THOCT IS FRE
KEEP VEILL THY TONGUE I COINSELL THE.

Sir Walter Scott quoted this in Chapter 25 of his *Fair Maid of Perth* wherein he comments that it was the belief that it alluded to the then abbot's mistress. The house is not open to the public.

The abbey's power added to the influence of the town which Alexander I had made a Burgh of Regality around 1124-27. The abbey had its ups and downs; it was largely destroyed by Edward I's forces in 1303, and its buildings were partly demolished by the Protestant reforming lords in 1560. The choir of the medieval church has completely disappeared, but the nave remains in the care of the Department of the Environment. The eastern part of the abbey had a new choir and transepts grafted onto it in 1818-21, and that part belongs to the Church of Scotland. Inside the modern church beneath the pulpit is sited the tomb of Robert I, the Bruce. He had been buried with great pomp in the abbey in 1329, but his tomb of white French marble had been destroyed by the Reformers. Above King Robert, one of Scotland's greatest rulers, had been this epitaph:

HIC JACET INVICTUS ROBERTUS, REX BENEDICTUS
QUI SUA GESTA LEGIT REPETAT QUOT BELLA PEREGIT
AD LIBERTATEM PERDUXIT PER PROBITATEM
REGNUM SCOTORUM: NUNC VIVAT IN ARCE POLORUM.

This might be rendered thus: 'Here lies the unconquered and blessed King Robert. Whosoever collects together [*the records of*] his warlike deeds, may recount what wars he prosecuted. He has led the Kingdom of the Scots through uprightness to liberty; now he lives in the Citadel of Heaven'. For five hundred years his tomb was lost, but when the ground was being cleared in 1818 for the new parish church, the site was rediscovered. A skeleton, presumed to be Bruce's, was discovered wrapped in cloth of gold; its breastbone had been split and this was deemed proof that it was Bruce's cadaver, as it was known that his heart had been removed, at his own request, so that it might be transported to the Holy Land on crusade. Bruce's heart now rests in its cone-shaped lead container in the floor of the chapter house of the Cistercian Abbey of Melrose. Bruce's tomb at Dunfermline is marked by a modern brass (1889) and is set in a base of Italian porphyry. ROBERTI DE BRUS SCOTORUM REGIS SEPULCHRUM. AD MDCCCXVIII INTER RUINAS PAVSTE RETECTUM HOC AERE DENVO CONSIGNATUM EST ANNO POST, PSIVS OBITUM DLX.

("The tomb of Robert Bruce, King of Scots, fortunately discovered among the ruins in 1818, has been marked anew by this brass in 560th year after his death").

Perhaps the worst desecration carried out by the Protestant Reformers at Dunfermline was that of the shrine of St Margaret, the site of which can still be seen behind the east gable of the modern church. Her relics remained intact until 1560, when Abbot George Durie took St Margaret's head to Edinburgh for safe keeping. In time the head was given to the Jesuits and transported to Antwerp in 1597, and there it remained until in 1645 it was transferred to the Scots College of Douai. The relics disappeared during the days of the French Revolution, although some of the saint's bones went to Spain.

Dunfermline Abbey was presented in 1589 to Anne of Denmark by James VI as a wedding present and in 1593 the buildings were annexed to the Crown in perpetuity. From the monastic guesthouse, refurbished by James V for his queen, there evolved the royal palace, and the unfortunate Charles I was born in the upper story of the west wing.

James VI it was who gave Dunfermline its Royal (confirming) Charter in 1588 and in 1624 the burgh was almost totally destroyed by fire. This contributed to the coming decline. As with St Andrews, the Reformation stripped Dunfermine of its importance as an ecclesiastical centre, and prosperity was not regained until weaving was introduced. The coming of the linen trade to Dunfermline was an interesting piece of industrial espionage. It seems that in the early 18th century a small damask-weaving manufacture was set up in Edinburgh by continental craftsmen. The damask process was secret, but in 1709, a Dunfermline weaver called James Blake absorbed the mysteries. He did this by impersonating an imbecile who hung around the looms of the immigrant weavers to amuse them. Blake was allowed to enter their workshops and as he capered for their pleasure he took note of both machines and processes. On returning to Dunfermline he was able to build his own industry. So weaving was established in the town by 1718 and the trade was revolutionised by the introduction of steam power in 1849. Today no linen is produced in the town and the old loom sheds have been either demolished or converted to other uses.

Dunfermline's District Museum in Viewfield Terrace chronicles in fine detail the history of the weaving and damask trade. By 1852 Dunfermline had settled into being, as the *Third Statistical Account of Fife* (1952) has it as 'a rather isolated, settled, self-centered community, composed predominantly of church-going, politically minded handloom weavers, with coal-mining taking place on the northern and western oustkirts of the burgh'; and those fundamental traits are still a part of the outlook of Dunfermline folk.

Today Dunfermline sits at the heart of a district with a population of 129,800. Silk is no longer woven in Dunfermline, but there is flourishing employment in engineering, electronics, papermaking, coal and construction.

Of Dunfermline's famous citizens Robert Henryson may be mentioned. He was a poet born in 1430 who came to the burgh to reside and take up employment as a schoolmaster. His writings range from the almost Chaucerian *Testament of Cresseid* to the humorous version he compiled of *Aesop's Fables.* But one does not go far in Dunfermline before coming across the name of Andrew Carnegie. He was born in Dunfermline in 1835 the son of a handloom weaver, and in 1848 his family emigrated to America and Andrew Carnegie passed from bobbin boy to telegraphic messenger, and thence to railroadman and entrepreneur in the iron and steel industry, to become the world's richest man. He sold the Carnegie Steel Company in 1901 and his personal share of the proceeds was £60,000,000. He set about spending his fortune on various public benefactions. His many gifts to Dunfermline included the Carnegie Baths (1877), the Library (1881) and scores of grants and donations. Andrew Carnegie's Birthplace in Moodie Street is a modern shrine to rival that of St Margaret in popularity. It is arranged today as a typical weaver's home and in the adjoining Memorial Hall there are exhibitions of the philanthropist's life and work. The Carnegie Dunfermline Trust sponsors the 'Dunfermline Heritage', and important stopping points on town walks are marked by their distinctive brown and cream plaques giving details of interesting buildings and locations. Thus the search for Carnegie, the Linen Weavers and Royal and Monastic Dunfermline is made easy.

Known locally as 'The Glen', Pittencrief Park is the real heart of Dunfermline. Tradition has it that as a boy Andrew Carnegie, who died in 1919, used to look with envy at the private policies of Pittencrieff House; he swore that one day he would be laird of Pittencrieff. He did just that and gifted the land and the house to his native burgh in 1903. The park now extends to 76 acres and offers a wide range of leisure, and recreational amenities, from an aviary to a model traffic area. Pittencrieff House was built around 1610 by Alexander Clerk; the house was renovated in 1911 under the eye of Sir Robert Lorimer. Herein are housed local history displays and exhibitions.

One of the distinctive features of Dunfermline are its City Chambers (1876-79) with the 117ft clock tower dominating the High Street. This was the successor of probably some four Town Houses, the first being destroyed in the fire of 1624; a later one stood on the present City Chambers site from 1771 to 1876. Dunfermline's Guildhall was built in 1807 by the Fraternity of Guildry, but was converted into a courthouse in 1848. Alongside New Row is Comely Park House (1785–restored 1893), headquarters of the Carnegie United Kingdom Trust.

III. Hill of Beath – Cowdenbeath – Lumphinnans – Lochgelly – Cardenden – Auchterderran – Kinglassie – Lochore – Ballingry – Kelty

Of all Fife's industries coalmining is the most ancient. As far back as 1291 the monastery at Dunfermline was granted a lease to exploit 'black stanes digged from the ground', and coalmining gave whole communities regular work and helped make the character of the people of West Fife. Indeed, Fife was once the largest coal-producing centre in Scotland and still today in the mining communities there is a doggedness of spirit, a ruggedness of independence, a toughness of character and a political loyalty which was forged at the coalface. This is the area which returned as MP the working-class agitator and Communist demagogue, William Gallagher (1881-1964), during 1935-50. West Fife's mining areas had less landowner influence too – despite such as the Earls of Minto and Zetland

The almost two centuries old Gothic-Italian style Tulliallan Castle, set within 90 acres of parkland, has been the home of the Scottish Police College since 1954. Extended in 1978, the college is unique in that it provides training in Junior, Senior, Detective and Traffic policework on one campus. The college contains historical displays of police items from all over the world *(Scottish Police College)*.

being superiors to Lochgelly and Ballingry respectively – social philanthropy coming from the efforts of local working people through such bodies as the Miners' Welfare groups. And women were given a prominent rôle too, as around a third of those employed, say, at Dunfermline's Baldridge colliery in the early 1800s were women. Their jobs included the heaving of the coal from the pit bottom to the surface; and often women worked underground with babies strapped to their backs. Coal is still a major activity in industrial Fife. A look at Fife's coal villages is well worth the effort and a round trip is easy from the M90, which helped to divert the slow-moving heavy goods vehicles through West and Central Fife.

From Junction 3 of the M90, the A970 leads east to the old mining village of Crossgates which is now bypassed; but there is still opencast coalmining in the area from the NCB headquarters at Crossgates. Rising to the west is the Hill of Beath, once clad with a birchwood forest, from which it takes its Gaelic name. The hollow in the hill's summit is the crater of a volcano, and from this vantage point the lookouts could warn the Covenanters at their secret services of the approach of soldiers. The Covenanters are continually referred to in Fife's story; these were the folk who had signed the Scottish National Covenant in 1638, supporting the Presbyterian religion against prelacy and popery.

When Queen Victoria passed through Cowdenbeath in 1842, on her first trip to Scotland, her entourage changed horses here. In those days the village was the centre of an agricultural region, with Cowdenbeath Inn an important coaching halt on the road north. Cowdenbeath, which became a burgh in 1890, began as a scattered agricultural community within a medieval barony. It has long been considered the 'capital' of the West Fife mining area and its prosperity has been closely linked to the vagaries of the coal industry. Iron ore first attracted miners here, but this was soon overhauled by the more profitable coal. There are still bitter memories of the Coal Strike of 1921 and of the General Strike of 1926, out of which the loyalty and solidarity of the miners has forged its own tradition.

The Kirk of Beath at Kirkton is reached from the centre of Cowdenbeath via Foulford Road and turning right into Old Perth Road. The present church was built in 1835-36 and added to in 1886, although there was a church here in the 12th century, and probably a Culdee chapel before that. The church lands hereabouts were conjointly held by the abbeys of Dunfermline and Inchcolm. The church has an octagonal bellcote and the manse was built in 1870. Its graveyard contains an interesting collection of headstone inscriptions and table tombs. The church also owned at least two mortsafes – those heavy coffin-shaped gratings used to guard the dead from the Resurrectionists; indeed the most immortal grusome twosome, William Burke and William Hare, are thought to have carried out a reconnoitre in the graveyard of Beath. The parish even got up a guard of farm workers to stand watch over the dead at the height of the grave-robbing scare.

Cowdenbeath Colliery Co (taken over by the Fife Coal Co in 1896) gave Lumphinnans its reason for existence, although

John Bleau's Atlas of 1654 shows a now vanished church by the burn. The hamlet retains its Public School buildings of 1892.

The A910 links all of the main mining areas in this district and leads on to Lochgelly. The records of Lochgelly, formerly a portion of the barony of Glassmount, go back to 1485 and it was once a market town for the local agricultural area, with a noted weaving centre. There was mining here from the 13th century by such as Sir John Wemyss of Wemyss; but even by the 16th century Lochgelly was still only a hamlet of thatched huts. Lochgelly was built up to house the workforce of the Lochgelly Iron and Coal Co, and ironstone was used in four great blast furnaces once sited near the railway station. The town became a burgh in 1876, and its pits are now closed. In the old days there was some rivalry between the weavers and the miners, the former thinking themselves of a 'better class'.

Lochgelly's name derived from the nearby eponymous loch once known for the efficacy of its leeches; today water sports have greater local fame. Lochgelly Curling Club was founded in 1831, preceding the foundation of the sport's governing body, the Royal Caledonian Curling Club (1838). Children once had reason to dislike the name Lochgelly as it was the commercial name of a locally made hard leather belt used in school for discipline. Children of eight years of age worked in the pits of early Victorian Lochgelly.

Miners' rows, now replaced with modern flats, were the homes of hundreds of families which earned a living since the Lochgelly Coal and Iron Co first started operations in 1850. Standing at 600 ft, Lochgelly is the highest township in Fife, and Wilson Street is probably one of the shortest streets anywhere. Lochgelly has seen many cultural changes, symbolised by the Lochgelly Centre (1976) for sports, arts, crafts and the theatre.

When the sale of liquor was restricted by the Forbes Mackenzie Act, crossed pipes in a Lochgelly shop meant that the shopkeeper was willing to slake the thirst of passers-by. Greyhounds and pigeon racing are the traditional pastimes of mining communities, but up to World War I at least Lochgelly offered a darker diversion – cockfighting, which had been illegal since 1849.

A famous daughter of Lochgelly is Baroness Lee of

Asheridge, the MP Jennie Lee of socialist legend; she was born at Lochgelly in 1904 the daughter of miner James Lee and served as MP for North Lanarkshire and in Staffordshire; in 1934 she married Aneurin Bevan (d.1960).

There is an atmosphere about Cardenden that still gives it the air of being a village. The modern layout takes in Cardenden itself, Auchterderran, Bowhill and Dundonald. Indeed the mining areas of Dundonald and Bowhill were, with Powguild, Balgreggie and Glenniston, within important medieval estates. This is the land of the Miners' Welfare system, and Bowhill Miners' Welfare Institute (1934) is a good example of its philosophy, for here is housed the local public library. The miners were always great readers and many of them tried their hands at writing. One well-remembered local writer was the poet Joe Corrie (1894-1968), who was generously described by T.S. Eliot as 'the greatest Scots poet since Burns'. The Communist Party once had great influence over this part of the mining community and local party members were the sponsors of a Burns Club that still exists today. The Bowhill People's Burns Club was established in 1940 and is one of the most active of the eleven Burns Clubs in Fife. They meet in the Gothenburg Suite of the Bowhill Public House Society, which in itself marks a Swedish public house system which was long associated with miners in West Fife. The profits from the pubs in the scheme were used for the benefit of the local community (funding electric lighting, a bowling green and so on).

Carden Tower, a mid-16th century building stands above the Carden burn within the Raith estate and was owned by the family of Mertyne of Medhope. The wild desolate area around Cardenden was once the haunt of gypsies, who became a recognised group in Fife by the 1450s. Gypsy lore asserts that they came to Fife from Ireland, and that they chose boggy, barren wastes so that pursuers might be slowed down.

A centrepiece of Auchterderran is its church dating from 1789, and it remains a typical example of Presbyterian austerity. Set in its choir is a 16th-century window from an earlier church, abutting the remnants of which is a memorial (1935) to the poet John Pindar (1837-1905). Pindar began work at ten years of age as a pony and cart driver at a pit in

Lochgelly. He became a soldier, and latterly served with the Highland Light Infantry and fought on the Northwest Frontier. Pindar's *Random Rhymes* were published in 1894. The poet's memorial stands near a fine doorway, with 1676 on its lintel. It is recorded that the land upon which the outbuildings of the church stand has a history going back to the 11th century when Fothad, Bishop of St Andrews, gave it to the monks of St Serf at Lochleven, when Auchterderran was callled Kirkindorath.

It is said that the very last duel in Scotland was acted out on 2 August 1826 in a field at Cardenbarns, Auchterderran. It took place between David Landale, a Kirkcaldy bleacher and merchant, and George Morgan, agent of the Bank of Scotland. Apparently Morgan had slandered Landale, and hit Morgan over the head with his umbrella. They decided to settle their differences through duelling with pistols, a pursuit that had been illegal since 1818 when an Act was passed in Parliament outlawing it. Morgan fired first, before time, and missed. Landale did not miss. Landale was arrested and sent for trial at Perth, but was acquitted. He lived in Kirkcaldy for many years after that and was a respected businessman.

The centre of an old hilly parish, Kinglassie was once a weaving village before the exploitation of coal. At nearby Whinnyhall, next to the B921 as it makes a sharp turn into Kinglassie, is the site of an invaders' fort, and in the marsh a Roman sword was found (1830). Once called Goatmilk, Kinglassie was given by Alexander I to the monks of Dunfermline; the old name is still retained by two farms and the hills abutting the golf course.

To the north of the village, on Redwell's Hill, stands the tower – visible for miles – known as 'Blythe's Folly'; the 52ft-high tower was set up in 1812 by an eccentric Leith shipowner. Two ancient estates are sited nearby. Inchdarvie had an early 15th-century mansion of 54 rooms owned by the Aytoun family, it was destroyed by fire in 1930. And Kinninmonth, once owned by a family of the same name, subsequently passed to the Earl of Minto. Just south of the B921 lies the Dogton Stone, an ancient Celtic Cross with traces of animal and figure sculpture. Entry to see it is free, via Dogton Farmhouse.

Today almost everyone in Ballingry, tucked under Benarty

Hill, is associated with the mining industry which wrought such enormous changes to the old 'Village of the Cross'. The origin of this strange nickname is likely to be entirely fanciful although it is quoted in the old *Statistical Account* with sincere authority. The story goes that the name is made up of *bal,* Gaelic for village, and *inri* spelling out *Iesus Nazarenus Rex Iudeorum* (Jesus of Nazareth, King of the Jews). It is more likely to come from the Gaelic *bal-an-righ,* the king's town.

The old village of Ballingry is represented by the ancient church and manse; remodelled in 1831, the church boasts of having been founded by missionaries sent from Lochleven by St Serf in the 6th century. It retains a two-tier square bellcote with knob finial. Sir Walter Scott mentions Ballingry's church in *The Abbot* (1820: chapter 33, 'Under your favour . . .'); he was a frequent visitor to the area from Blairadam, and his elder son Walter married the heiress Jane Jobson of Lochore House.

Among all the mining communities in West Fife, perhaps Lochore more than any other suffered the worst environmental pollution from the coal companies. The loch which gave the town its name was drained for agricultural purposes in 1792, but in the early 1900s sludge lagoons built up in its old bed, and black heaps of waste piled up and the area was totally spoiled. In the 1980s a concerted effort was made to give the countryside around Lochore a spectacular facelift and the dereliction was swept away. The centrepiece of the area now is the Lochore Meadows Country Park, where leisure activities from sailing to ornithology are catered for on the shore of Dunfermline District's largest loch, Loch Ore. Tempted by the new habitats, wildlife has reappeared in the area which is patrolled by park rangers and visitor guides. The 260-acre loch is well stocked with brown trout throughout the year.

From the park centre nature trails fan out to the main features. Once on its own island of Inchgall (the Isle of Strangers), Lochore Castle was built in 1160 by the Norman Duncan de Lochore. This remained the home for succeeding families like the Valances who added to the original motte and bailey, until John Malcolm of Balbedie purchased it; in the 17th century the Malcolm family abandoned the castle and built Lochore House further up the hill beyond the golf course.

no more

The pit winding gear of the Mary Pit, which closed in 1966, stands in the park as a memory of the great days of mining. The park may be reached from the B920, turning in at Lochore church.

Kelty stands right on the northern edge of Dunfermline District and is skirted by the old county boundary as it crosses the M90 to make for Benarty Hill; the town is also reached by the A903 from Cowdenbeath. It was Kelty that was to see the formation in 1872 of the Fife Coal Co which was to play such an important part in the lives of the West Fife miners. The colliery's main acquisition were: Hill of Beath (1887); Cowdenbeath (1896); Lochore and Capledrae (1900); Blairadam (1901); and Bowhill (1909). The collieries, lands and properties were nationalised in 1946.

To the west of Kelty, across the M90, lies Blairadam Forest, of which over two-thirds lie in Fife. The setting up of forestry in this area dates back to 1733 when the famous Scottish architect William Adam purchased the estate of The Blair and built Blairadam House (over the border in Perthshire). During 1739-47 neighbouring estates were added and the Adams began a pioneer afforestation on treeless country for commercial timber; most of this was felled in the two World Wars. The Forestry Commission have replanted mostly Sitka and Norway spruces and have supplied clearly marked forest picnic areas which are reached from the B914.

William Adam's grandson, William, was Lord Chief Commissioner of the Jury Court, and he and his friend Sir Walter Scott founded the Blairadam Club in 1816, whose purpose was from time to time to visit local sites of historical or literary interest. From Blairadam Scott set out on his expeditions into Fife. Here it was too that Sir Walter Scott's anonymity was unmasked as the author of the 'Waverley' novels; the knoll in the park over which the Blairadam Club members often walked was called Kiery Crags by Sir Walter in his book *The Abbot.*

IV. Saline – Blairhall – Comrie – Oakley – Carnock

From Kelty the B914 takes a direct route west out of Fife into Clackmannan District, through the mining village of Steelend given birth by the Wilson & Clyde Coal Co, to Saline, the largest town in northwest Fife. A detour to the right where the B914 crosses the A823 leads to the Motor Racing Circuit on Dunfermline District's 'roof' at Knockhill (which rises to over 1180 ft above sea-level) and access to the Cleish Hills favoured by ramblers. In fact the whole of this area offers well-marked short and long walks.

Saline provides superb views of the Ochil Hills and it is a good place to reflect on Fife's geology. The Ochils are a huge mass of andesite, igneous rock of the Old Red Sandstone period, and in the region of Saline (and the rock south of the Ochils) there are softer sedimentary rocks of the upper Old Red Sandstone era. All the rest of Fife is made up of carboniferous rock, overlaid in some places such as Saline with dolerite sills and penetrated volcanic intrusions (Saline Hill at 1178 ft; Benarty Hill at 1167 ft and so on). The township of Saline was long a royal 'gift' apportioned to that member of the Royal Family who held the title of the Earl of Mar. In spite of ironstone and coalmining activities Saline does retain some 'old-fashioned' charm with its 18th and 19th-century dwellings, and is known for its heavily ornamented cottages with their castellated gateways, the work of the stonemason family of Mercer. The present church was built in 1810 on a pre-Reformation site; many of the stones of the old church were built into the house of Devonview. Sir Walter Scott was a frequent visitor to Saline, staying at Nether Kinneddar, with William Erskine, Lord Kinneddar of Session. Scott dedicated the third Canto of *Marmion* (1808) to Erskine, who is credited with the preface to *The Bridal of Triermain.* (1813).

The A907 runs south of Saline to Dunfermline and is linked to it by the B913. Along the A907 are an interesting series of villages worth more than just a glance. Blairhall is one of Fife's youngest villages which developed to house the miners of the colliery founded in 1911. Comrie serves a relatively modern colliery dating from 1936. And Oakley once had six blast furnaces for its flourishing Oakley Iron Works started in 1846,

Culross, with its dignified 16th-century Mercat Cross, lies on the north shore of the River Forth. The most remarkable example of a small Scottish town of the 16th and 17th centuries, little has changed at Culross for 300 years, although the town has been extensively restored by the National Trust for Scotland and others. Behind the Mercat Cross stands the crowstepped Study of c.1610, with corbelled Outlook Tower where, tradition has it, Bishop Leighton of Dunblane studied in the 17th century *(D.C. Thomson & Co Ltd)*.

but now it is a quiet mining settlement. The community grew in the 1930s and 1940s after the sinking of the Comrie mine and developed following the arrival of many Roman Catholic miners from the ailing Lanarkshire coalfields. The village has a white harled Roman Catholic church of interest; the Church of the Most Holy Name (1956-58) has notable stained-glass windows from France, and notable too are the wood block Stations of the Cross.

Carnock is a place to pause and take in the delineation of West Fife, for old and new Carnock offer a tilted view of the landscape. Here are the ruins of a 12th-century church from which it is said the village derives its name – St Cearnock was one of the disciples of St Ninian who brought Christianity to Scotland in the 4th century. It is possible that this church belonged to the Trinitarians, the 'Red Friars' of Scotlandwell, Kinross. In the 17th century Sir George Bruce was one of the foremost of Fife's salt manufacturers and he had mining interests in these parts. The old church of Carnock was erected by Sir George in 1602 to replace the earlier edifices; much more of Sir George's architectural inspiration can be seen at Culross. The manse of Carnock was built and repaired 1742-81. The present church was built in 1840 and 'improved' in 1894. At the east end of the old churchyard can be found the grave of Rev. John Row (d.1646), a prominent Presbyterian who organised Communion Services; while at Carnock he wrote his *History of the Kirk.*

V. Kincardine – Tulliallan – Culross – Valleyfield – Newmills – Torrybury – Cairneyhill – Crossford – Crombie – Charlestown – Limekilns – Pattiesmuir – Rosyth

The Kingdom of Fife may be entered from the west via the A977 for Alloa, or on the A876 which crosses the Forth just south of Airth. With its former two thriving shipbuilding yards, Kincardine-on-Forth was once one of the most important harbours on the upper Forth. But the days when nearly one hundred vessels were registered in Kincardine have gone. Up to 1906, when Dunfermline-Alloa branch railway line was opened, Kincardine was something of a backwater, difficult to get to despite the ferries, for its roads were narrow and twisting and the bridal paths inconvenient.

A focal point of modern Kincardine still remains the swing bridge, opened in 1936, and deemed 'one of the wonders of the 20th century'; the bridge carries the A876 into the heart of the town. At 2696 ft long, the bridge's central swing span was powered by two 50hp electric motors, which moved it through a full 90 degree swing. In 1988 the swing bridge became permanently fixed.

There are still some interesting examples of Scottish domestic architecture in Kincardine and the impressive mercat cross is worthy of a look. But the shoreline by the bridge is dominated by Kincardine Power Station. The station was formally opened in 1960, but was not completed until 1963. It stands on land reclaimed from the Forth in 1822. Of Kincardine's famous sons, Sir James Dewar (1842-1923) may be remembered – he invented the vacuum flask.

Tulliallan is Kincardine's neighbour on the edge of the curiously named Devilla Forest, with its Moor Loch and Peppermill Dam. Once, with Culross Moor, it was a wild place, the sanctuary of outlaws and ne'er-do-wells. There are the remains of a hill fort at Castle Hill, south of the A907, by Bogside, and stone coffins and urns of prehistoric date were located (in 1856 and 1934) at Tulliallan Nursery. Near to Peppermill Dam is the Landsdowne family mausoleum. They were descendants of the Keiths who came to own Tulliallan, and the site of the mausoleum was formely a pre-Reformation parish church.

It is said that the Forth almost washed the walls of the ruined Tulliallan castle at Hawkhill, once the home of the Blackadders. The castle was already a strong fortress when Edward I invaded Scotland in the 13th century. The estate was bought by Admiral Viscount Keith in 1798. The castle had probably been abandoned as a home in the early 17th century and a modern mansion was built in 1818 by Admiral George Keith Elphinstone, a one-time serving officer with Lord Nelson. Today the Gothic-Italian mansion is the heart of The Scottish Police College. The property was bought in 1950 and the first courses started in 1954. Much modernisation and renovation have taken place; the mansion's stables and garages at Blackhall were converted for driver training in 1964, while the most recent extention was to the classroom, library and study bedroom complex in 1978.

The old parish church of Tulliallan abutting the estate was

unroofed when replaced by the present church of 1833; but the bell-tower dates from 1675. The old graveyard reflects the seafaring nature of the ancient community with its symbols of death interspersed with ships in sail.

The west coastland of Fife can be explored as far as the Forth Bridges by way of the B9037, which with the railway as a companion hugs the north shore of the Forth. Fed by the railway and the nearby slip roads, Longannet Power Station dominates the shoreline reclaimed from the Forth, using ash from Kincardine Power Station. The station at Longannet Point produces half the electricity in Central Scotland; its four 600-megawatt generators produce three million horsepower from five million tons of coal annually. About half of this coal is delivered direct by the National Coal Board's specially constructed mine complex located within the power station's site. The power station, with its 600ft-high single chimney, was begun in 1964 and remains the largest power station in operation in Britain.

Before arriving at Culross the B9037 passes the castles of Blair and Dunimarle. Blair houses the Charles Carlow (1848-1923) Memorial Home for Miners, founded by the Fife Coal Co and named after their erstwhile Chairman and Managing Director. Dunimarle is a fake castle which is supposed to have been on the site of the castle in which Lady Macduff and her children were murdered; the castle museum is open to the public at set times.

A programme of imaginative restoration by the National Trust for Scotland, the Department of the Environment and others has assured the preservation of Culross's essential charm. For here, conserved for all time, is an attractive small Scottish burgh of the 17th and 18th centuries with a wealth of Scottish vernacular architecture.

The Royal Burgh of Culross was the legendary birthplace of St Kentigern (St Mungo to Glaswegians), following his mother Princess Thenew's flight in disgrace from her father the King of Lothian's wrath. She had been cast adrift at Aberlady in an open boat and left to perish. The wind and tide miraculously brought her to the shore at Culross, and her landing place was commemorated in 1503 when Glasgow's first archbishop, Robert Blackadder, set up St Mungo's chapel.

Here St Kentigern was brought up by St Serf and sent forth to spread the gospel himself. Culross's importance was assured when in 1217 Malcolm, 7th Earl of Fife, founded the abbey on the hill for the Cistercian monks of Kinloss, Moray. These monks were famed for their calligraphy and illumination and the *Culross Psalter* (in the National Library of Scotland in Edinburgh) is a fine example of their work. Dedicated to the Blessed Virgin, St Andrew and St Serf, the abbey fell into secular hands at the Reformation. The parish church of Culross occupies the site of the monk's choir and has been used as such since 1633; the church was modernised in 1824. All visitors should make time to look at the unusual (to survive) tomb (1642) of Sir George Bruce, with its alabaster effigies of himself, his wife Margaret and their eight children. Culross Abbey House was begun by Sir Edward Bruce in 1608; it was remodelled in 1830 and reconstructed by the Earl of Elgin in 1955.

During the 16th century salt panning, coal mining and trade with the Low Countries were the burgh's principal activities, and the foreshore port of Sandhaven ensured prosperity. One of Culross's famous products was the now rare iron baking girdles; James VI re-established the town's Hammermen's monopoly of their manufacture in 1599. Decline set in at Culross when political and economic influence moved to Central and Western Scotland, and the burgh was almost forgotten until the 1930s when the restoration programme was begun.

Today Culross is an architectural feast of dormer windows, skewputts, decorative lintels and crow-stepping. A couple of hours' wander around Culross is richly rewarding, but it is a place to visit more than once. Along the Sandhaven, which flanks the Forth and forms the site of the old shore port, is the Townhouse built in 1626; its steeple was added in 1783 and the lower floor was a prison called the Laigh Tolbooth; in front of this is the Tron, the site of the public weighbeam. Incidentally a 'Culross chalder' was the standard Scottish measure for weighing coal. Along from the Tolbooth is the Palace, built by the merchant and entrepreneur Sir George Bruce between 1597 and 1611. Its name derives from the Latin *palatium* – or Hall – and does not signify any royal connections, although

James VI did stay at Culross Palace in 1617. Sir George's name is featured a great deal in the history of West Fife, for his mining activities were famous; he installed an ingenious apparatus to drain his mines and he is credited with sinking the first mine under the sea.

Near the Palace is the Bessie Bar Hall and Well. Bessie Bar was a 16th-century personage who sold malt; the well was constructed by the Council in 1598. From Sandhaven the Back Causeway leads into Tanhouse Brae and the 'House with the Evil Eyes' (so called from the shape of its windows in the Dutch gable), west of the parish church. In Tanhouse Brae are a former sea-captain's dwelling, the 'House of the Greek Inscription', which spells out 'God provides and will provide', and the Snuff-Makers's House of 1673. Round the window of Snuff Cottage is the inscription 'Wha wad ha' thocht it'; the second line of this old jingle, 'Noses wad ha' bought it', was on another snuff-maker's house in Edinburgh. In the Back Causeway is 'The Study' of 1610 with its oak panelling dating from 1633. This is said to have been used by Bishop Leighton of Dunblane on his visitations. Immediately below the outlook tower of the Bishop's study is The Haggs, or Stinking Wynd, whose camber recalls an interesting social custom of past days. The centre of the cobbled way is several inches higher than its edges; this was 'the croon o' the causie' (causeway) where local well-to-do folk walked . . . the poor gave way in the gutters.

Parallel with Back Causeway is Mid Causeway with Bishop Leighton's Lodgings, his refuge in troubled ecclesiastical times. Wee Causeway contains the Nunnery, which takes its name from the veiled head of a woman carved on the lower end of the crow-stepped gable. All the causeways lead to the Mercat Cross which originates from 1588 and was restored in 1910.

The next community encountered after Culross is Valleyfield, now developed into the mining settlement of High Valleyfield, which sits on the hill above the older Low Valleyfield. The estate of Valleyfield belonged to Sir Robert Preston who employed Humphry Repton (1752-1818), one of the great 'legends' of the English art of landscape gardening, to improve his parkland. Preston's house was demolished in 1918 and much of Repton's landscaping is irredeemably lost, destroyed by its later owner, the East Fife Coal Co, who bought

HM Naval Base, Rosyth, was created after the Admiralty bought 1248 acres of land on the north shore of the Forth in 1903. A town was built around the Royal Navy Dockyard to house the yard's workers and their families. Rosyth's population today is about 13,000. The Naval Base is open to the public every June to view British and Allied warships.

the estate in 1907 for its mineral rights. Valleyfield is still remembered in mining lore for the pit disaster of 1939 when 35 miners lost their lives. Look for the recently restored 'Endowment', built by Sir Robert Preston for a dozen pensioners.

The Bluther Burn runs under the B9037 at Newmills which gets its name from the mill which once stood here. Formerly a part of Perthshire, this was the site of the monkish *Novum Molendinium* which had the monopoly of the grinding of all grain in the vicinity.

Witch mania was once rife in Torryburn and many an unfortunate demented soul was consigned to the flames along these shores; on the foreshore by the railway bridge stands a rock with the remains of an iron ring associated with Lilias Adie, who in 1704 was the last Torryburn witch; she was buried here by the high watermark. Standing above a fast-moving burn, Torryburn and Newmills parish church was built in 1800 and reconstructed in 1928. Its hexagonal bellcote stands above an outside stairway leading to the choir loft, and at its gate is an interesting watchhouse. The table tombs in the graveyard are worthy of a note for their symbols.

A mile offshore lies Preston Island in Torry Bay, where Sir Robert Preston of Valleyfield (d.1834) sank three pits; they were abandoned in 1811 after a fatal explosion.

From the time of the Reformation the churches of Torryburn and Crombie were associated and in 1622 the parishes were united. The present church of Crombie was built in 1800 on the site of older foundations. As with all Fife churchyards, it is well worth exploring for its 18th-century inscriptions. Here's a famous epitaph from Crombie:

> In this churchyard lies Eppie Coutts,
> Either here or hereabouts.
> But whaur it is nane can tell
> Till Eppie rise and tell hersel'.

The small oblong ruin in the churchyard is probably 13th century and has long been used as a vault for the Colville family. A native of Torryburn was Alison Cunningham, born here in 1822, she became nanny to Robert Louis Stevenson and is immortalised in the dedication of *A Child's Garden of Verses* (1885); she died at Edinburgh in 1910 aged 92.

Outside Cairneyhill the B9037 joins the A985 and A994. If the visitor takes the latter towards Dunfermline, Cairneyhill is first encountered. This is an old weavers' village, now a dormitory village for Dunfermline. To the west lies Conscience Brig, so called because a murderer is said to have confessed his crime here.

Next comes Crossford. The ford crossed by the monks on their way between the abbeys of Dunfermline and Culross is long gone, but Crossford retains its main street of old houses. Once a busy weaving and market garden community thrived here on land distributed by the drawing of lots. This was called *cavelling* the land, and it probably derives from nearby Keavil House (a medieval mansion now converted into a modern hotel) on whose estates large housing developments have taken place.

Just before the A994 leads into Crossford, on the right is the golf course and Pitfirrane estate. For centuries Pitfirrane was the mansion of the Halkett family, and when Miss Madeline Halkett died in 1951 the house and grounds were purchased by the Carnegie Trust and now form the clubhouse and course of the Dunfermline Golf Club. The buildings seen today are largely of the late 16th century, but the core of Pitfirrane is the 15th-century L-plan tower. The south wing was added in the 17th century and the castle yett now forms the gate leading to the gardens. The house retains fine armorial ceilings in two public rooms.

If the A985 is taken towards Rosyth, the visitor comes to Crombie and the second part of West Fife's shoreline. The warships from Rosyth Dockyard now receive their ordance at Crombie, but once passenger ships called here on their way up and down the river from Leith to Stirling.

It is not often that someone perpetuates his name in the layout of a village. In the 1750s, Charles, 5th Earl of Elgin, in seeking to expand his business interests, opened a limestone quarry, built kilns and laid out a harbour and model village. The village of Charlestown, which lies to the south of the modern A985, was set out in the shape of a great letter E. Still along the shore at Charlestown is the largest group of limekilns in Scotland – 14 in all – which processed the lime exported all over Scotland. Limestone from here too built the docks at Dundee and Leith.

Between Charlestown and Limekilns lies Broomhall House, the seat of the Earls of Elgin and Kincardine, and it is set out on lands once owned by the monastery at Dunfermline. In the Middle Ages the estate was known as Gedeleth and was acquired in 1562 by Robert Richardson, Treasurer to Mary, Queen of Scots. The property was purchased in 1600 by Sir George Bruce, who changed the name to Broomhall. It was Thomas, 7th Earl of Elgin (1766-1841), who secured the marbles from the Parthenon when he was Ambassador-Extraordinary in Turkey; as 'the Elgin Marbles' they were placed in the British Museum in 1816. Today the Earl of Elgin remains the nearest male relative to the line of Robert I, the Bruce, and at Broomhall are retained relics of the famous king; a large two-handed sword and a helmet are displayed, both said to have been borne by Bruce at the Battle of Bannockburn in 1314. Broomhall is not open to the public.

Once press-gangs roamed the ancient thoroughfares of the seaport of Limekilns on the lookout for likely seamen to serve on the grain, wood and lime ships of the Limekilns fleet. But nowadays piers like Capernaum serve as moorings for the sailing club. Limekilns formerly had a soap and rope works, saltpans and a brewery, and in Academy Square the King's Cellar stored provisions for the Palace of Dunfermline. Its doorway of 1581 bears the arms of the Commendator of Dunfermline, Robert Pitcairn. Robert Louis Stevenson (1850-94) had David Balfour and Alan Breck of his novel *Kidnapped* (1886) stop at the Ship Inn to beg food and a passage across the Forth.

Among the handful of buildings at the mini-hamlet of Pattiesmuir there is to be found a 'college', the social meeting place for weavers, once chaired by Andrew Carnegie's grandfather as 'professor'; but nothing remains of the Palace of the King of the Gypsies who once sojoured here. It is today a place of pleasant walks in the wooded countryside.

The A985 leads on to the town of Rosyth which was created in 1903 when the Admiralty bought land here for a naval base. The foreshore has long been known as St Margaret's Hope, the place where Margaret Atheling landed in 1069. On this peninsula is set Rosyth Castle, now surrounded by the off-limits paraphernalia of the dock. The castle was used as a seaside resort by Mary, Queen of Scots, who later embarked from the peninsula of Rosyth Castle after her escape from Lochleven Castle in 1568. Its chief feature today is the massive 15th-century Tower House, which was both fortress and home; it fell to Cromwell's soldiers in 1651. Indeed there is a tradition that Oliver Cromwell's mother was born in the castle. Queen Victoria remarked on the tradition in her *Leaves from the Journal of our Life in the Highlands* (1867), when she remembered embarking on the little steamer for North Queensferry during her visit of 1842. It is a story however that is easily exploded. Cromwell's mother was Elizabeth Lyon, daughter of William Steward (from Stywood not the royal Stewarts) of Ely, Cambridgeshire, whose family had founded their wealth on the fall of the Roman Catholic Church.

A.J. Balfour's Conservative government finally decided to

build a dockyard at Rosyth in 1903; it was to be a complete repair establishment capable of taking the *Dreadnought* class of battleship. The dockyard stands on reclaimed land and construction began in 1909; the first vessel to be repaired in the graving docks was HMS *Zealandia* which entered No 1 Dock in March 1916. Submarines, then known as K craft, first came to Rosyth in 1917. Between the wars Rosyth was placed on a 'care and maintenance' basis – although a large number of vessels of the German High Seas Fleet were broken up here in the 1920s; the base was re-activated in 1939.

The naval base has been developed steadily since World War II and is by far the largest employer of labour in Fife; the main stream of work is refitting nuclear Polaris and conventional submarines, frigates, mine countermeasure ships, offshore protection vessels and numerous auxiliary vessels. The Royal Naval Base also includes HMS *Cochrane* (1968) as a Fleet Accommodation Centre for the Rosyth Area, and HMS *Caledonia* (1979) is an Apprentice Training Establishment.

Flag Officer Scotland and Northern Ireland is located at the Maritime HQ at Pitreavie Castle, once the home of the Wardlaw family; the castle dates from around 1615. Pitreavie is the nerve centre of naval and air operations in the North Atlantic, and close to its walls the last blows were meted out in 1651 when the Commonwealth Army under Oliver Cromwell defeated the Scots supporting Charles II. A prominent owner of Pitreavie was Sir Henry Wardlaw (d.1638), chamberlain to James VI's consort, Anne of Denmark.

CHAPTER 2

Kirkcaldy and Industrial South Fife

I. The Lang Toun – Kirkcaldy

Thomas Carlyle (1795-1881), the Scottish author and sage of peasant stock, who lodged at 22 Kirk Wynd, knew Kirkcaldy well. He said of the burgh that it was 'A mile of smoothest sand, with one long wave coming on gently, steadily and breaking in gradual explosion into harmless white, the breaking of it melodiously rushing along like a mass of foam, beautifully sounding and advancing from the West Burn to Kirkcaldy Harbour'. Much has changed in Kirkcaldy since Carlyle's time, but the shops and houses are still set along the deep rim of a shallow bay which traces the cause of the burgh's nickname, 'The Lang Toun'. Kirkcaldy's main thoroughfare is still some four miles long, from Linktown, through Pathhead to Sinclairtown and Gallatown. And today with a population of 49,820 Kirkcaldy is the largest town in Fife and is the administrative centre of Kirkcaldy District.

Kirkcaldy's policies once formed one of the most ancient burghs in Scotland when David II handed it over to the monks of Dunfermline in 1364, who in turn gave it over in 1450 to the baillies and community of Kirkcaldy. Charles I ratified all the privileges of the burgh in 1644 and in 1661 his son Charles II did the same and made Kirkcaldy a royal burgh. The burgh developed from its main street and harbour, and the Teil (West) Burn, noted by Carlyle, is now dominated by the massive pit area and marshalling yard of Seafield Colliery, which since 1954 has been one of Fife's largest remaining collieries. In Carlyle's day too the ruin of Seafield Tower, threatened by the colliery perimeter, would be a pastoral stroll away. This square tower built on igneous rock by the sea was the home of the Moutrays (see page 32). The nearby Partan Rocks – so named for crabs could be scooped from them at high tide – were designated in 1953 by the Nature Conservancy Council as 'of special geological interest', as are the coral fossils of Hoch-ma-toch inlet. On the hill, across the railway, stands

Abden Home, once a Victorian Poor Law House, which has been converted into flats.

Modern Kirkcaldy has a highly diversifed industrial base, but its street names proclaim its industrial past, from Coal Wynd (the route of coal transported from Lina Pit to the harbour) to Nairn Street (remembering the family who made floor coverings), and from Pottery Street (from the Gallatown Pottery) to Prime Gilt Box Street. The latter has a fascinating derivation from *prymgilt,* the first anchorage of a ship using a port. The Prime Gilt Box Society of Kirkcaldy was a charity for dependants of mariners lost at sea.

The invention of linoleum made Kirkcaldy the 'oil cloth capital', despite such of the burgh's older trades as textiles (Kirkcaldy was the first town to have a powerloom in operation in 1821), early salt panning, engineering, chemical factories and rope works. Linoleum is the name given to a specific type of floor covering invented in 1860 by Englishman Frederick Watson. It forms a hard-surfaced, pliable floor covering prepared by pressing or calendaring a plastic mass in a smooth sheet. The plastic mass is derived initially from linseed oil. It was the linseed oil that gave Kirkcaldy its distinctive aroma, immortalised by Mrs George Smith of Kirkcudbrightshire, whose poem 'The Boy in the Train' contains the couplet:

> For I ken' mysel' by the queer-like smell,
> That the next stop's Kirkcaldy.

Kirkcaldy's floorcloth industry was developed from 1847 by a weaver of canvas called Michael Nairn (1804-58), who had diversified from weaving ships' sails to manufacturing a backing for floorcloth. In 1849 Nairn was making his own floorcloth and out of his enterprise, Watson's invention, and the patronage of the working class who favoured lino, there sprang Michael Nairn & Co Ltd, which provided a multitude of employment; the Nairn family became great benefactors to the burgh, gifting such beneficies as a Cottage Hospital (1890) and a school (1894 – now part of Kirkcaldy College of Technology).

Today the industrial estates of Hayfield, Mitchelston and Randolph generate much of Kirkcaldy's modern wealth. The whole panoply of Kirkcaldy's industrial history is housed in exhibitions in the Kirkcaldy Industrial Museum next to the railway station. The early industries, incidentally, are commented on in the introductory part of John Buchan's *Free Fishers.* Born at Perth, Buchan (1875-1940) spent a part of his early youth in Kirkcaldy at Pathhead where his father was minister; his sister Anna (novelist O. Douglas) was born in Kirkcaldy.

Two leisurely saunters can give the visitor the flavour of modern Kirkcaldy set in its past. In one the town centre may be explored and in the other the shore and harbour.

The harbour area is a good place to start a stroll around Kirkcaldy, remembering though that the harbour belongs to the Forth Ports Authority and access is restricted. The inner dock was constructed in 1904 to expedite cargoes of coal and linoleum; once the whalers of the North Atlantic fleet docked here. The buildings of Robert Hutchinson & Co Ltd, maltsters and millers, still dominate the harbour. Opposite the harbour is Sailors' Walk. Built around 1460, it is the oldest house in Kirkcaldy; Charles II rested here in 1650 as he passed through the town after his coronation at Scone. Now the Customs House, the building is very Dutch in influence with its pantiles, crow-stepping and windowed gables. This part of the High Street is a place of many wynds – the old Scots word for alley. Near to the harbour was the area of the old salt pans where Oswald of Dunnikier extracted salt from sea water.

Most of the houses in the High Street, of Victorian and Edwardian date, are much altered, but several are noteworthy, like the Swan Memorial of 1905 built in memory of Provost Don Swan (1808-89), friend of Thomas Carlyle. On the wall of the savings bank is a plaque noting that Thomas Carlyle 'lodged here 1816-19' when he was a teacher at the now vanished Burgh School in Hill Street. Up the brae of Kirk Wynd is Kirkcaldy's 'Old Kirk'. the original church was consecrated in 1244 and its Norman tower is all that is left of the pre-Reformation edifice; the church was rebuilt in 1807, and its interior refurbished in 1968. At the top of Kirk Wynd is St Brycedale Church (1877-78) with its distinctive 200ft spire; it took its name from the patron saint of Kirkcaldy and the nearby estate on which it was built.

At No 220 High Street (The Pend) lived the famous Scottish

economist Adam Smith (1723-90), whose *Inquiry into the nature and causes of the Wealth of Nations* (1776) has never been out of print.

Tolbooth Street recalls the old town hall rebuilt in 1678; here was located the town jail – a new Tolbooth was built in 1826 and served the community until 1953. It is interesting to note whenever a Fife town jail is being researched that imprisonment was never in high favour as a form of punishment for most offences; up to the living memory of Victorians, hanging, scourging, and banishment were favoured punishments. Long-term imprisonment was not popular amongst local baillies and many a Kirkcaldy miscreant would have had his ear nailed to a post hereabouts . . . there he, or she, would be left until courage was plucked up to tear the head away.

Opposite the site of the Tolbooth, and set in the street, is a large red cross, said to have marked the site of the old Mercat Cross, removed in 1782. (Local historians believe that the cross is more likely to have marked the site of an earlier Tolbooth.) In the vicinity of the Mercat Cross would be kept the public weights and a Tron, or weight-beam. In medieval Fife at least three standards of weight would be in use: English pounds (16 oz), Dutch pounds (17½ oz) and Tron pounds (22 oz). English measures were used to weigh out flour, bread and barley; Dutch for meat and meal; and Tron weights for flax, wool, butter, cheese and tallow. Gone too are the names of some of the old measures, from *lippie* (2lbs) to *firlot* (2 stone).

At No 132 High Street the remarkable Marjorie Fleming was born in 1803. Although she died at the age of eight, her journal *Pet Marjorie* (1858) became cult reading. She is buried in Abbotshall churchyard, where her life-size effigy shows the famous journal open on her knee.

Off High Street is Glassworks Street where Sir Sandford Fleming was born in 1827; he became Chief Engineer of the Canadian Pacific Railway and the inventor of Standard Time, accepted internationally from 1883.

Further along Nicol Street is Bethelfield Church (1831); from a predecessor of which issued one day in 1778 the Rev Robert Shirra who, assembling with his parishoners on the beach, called upon the Almighty to stop the threatened pillage of the town by the pirate John Paul Jones; it is said a storm blew up and Jones had to abandon his plans.

Running almost parallel with High Street is Kirkcaldy's mile-long Esplanade, beginning at its west end at Linktown where was located Gladney House, the home of the Adam family of architects; Robert Adam was born at Kirkcaldy in 1728. For a week in April the Esplanade is thronged with crowds who come to the Links Market; Kirkcaldy's Easter Chartered Fair was recognised as early as 1305. Today the event is a cacophanous gathering of colourful carousels and the cries of barkers. The Esplanade was built in 1922-23 to relieve unemployment and keep back the sea.

The railway station, built in 1964 to replace the one of 1847, is a convenient start to a gentle exploration of the centre of Kirkcaldy. Opposite are the War Memorial Gardens and the Art Gallery, Museum and Public Library gifted by John Nairn in the 1920s. Across the gardens, at the corner of Bennochy Rd and St Brycedale Avenue, is the Adam Smith Centre; this was the old Adam Smith Hall (1899), funded as a public amenity by Andrew Carnegie; the Hall was renovated in 1973 and today is the centre of cultural activities. Down Abbotshall Road (under the railway bridge) stands Abbotshall Church and graveyard; traditionally called 'the Kirk on the Knoll', the sandstone building dates from 1790, replacing earlier churches; the crypt is said to date from the 8th century.

Kirkcaldy's Town House (1953/56) lies in Town Square, formerly the site of some fine large town houses. In the foyer of the Town Hall is the Town Bell and a memorial to 'Six Famous Sons of Kirkcaldy': Robert Adam (1728-92); Sir Sandford Fleming (1827-1915); Dr John Philp (1775-1851), missionary in South Africa; Baillie Robert Philp (1751-1828), linen manufactuer and educational benefactor; Adam Smith (1723-90); and John McDouall Stuart (1815-66), explorer of the Australian interior. The Town House known colloquially by local politicians as 'The Big Hoose' also features Walter Pritchard's mural telling the story of Kirkcaldy. Behind the Town Hall are the Provosts' Lamps, which were set here when the six local burghs united in 1975 to form Kirkcaldy District Council. At the top of Whytecauseway is the Scottish Baronial-style Sheriff Court, whose original building dates from 1894.

This postcard picture shows what Kirkcaldy harbour looked like at the turn of the 19th century. Facing the Inner Harbour is the crowstepped 'Sailor's Walk', the oldest house in Kirkcaldy, built *circa* 1460. The site of the sheds to the right of the picture is now dominated by the premises of Robert Hutchinson & Co Ltd, maltsters and millers.

Kirkcaldy sports a number of fine parks. At 'the back o' the toon' is Dunnikier Park on the A988 (Dunnikier Way) set out on the policies of the estate owned by the Oswald family, and offering a full-size municipal golf course and nature trail. Dunnikier House was built in 1791.

Beveridge Park is reached via Abbotshall Road from the centre of town. It was gifted to Kirkcaldy by Michael Beveridge (1836-90), a floorcovering manufacturer and prominent Kirkcaldy benefactor. It lies next to the policies of Raith House, erected in 1694 by Lord Raith, son of the first Earl of Melville. The parkland is now bisected by the B925 (Boglily Road) to Auchtertool, but once the grassland was all of a piece; the lodge (1790) by the gateway to Beveridge Park was the main entrance to Raith House.

Running past Beveridge park is Balwearie Road, which reminds us of a famous name in Kirkcaldy's history. For, in the tower house of Balwearie lived Sir Michael Scott. (c.1160-1235), the philosopher who lives in folklore as 'a wizard' largely through the allusions about him in Walter Scott's *The Lay of the Last Minstrel* (1805). The Italian poet Dante mentioned the wizard in his *Inferno:*

> That other there, whose ribs fill scanty space
> Was Michael Scott, who truly full well knew
> Of magical deceits the illusive grace.

To the west of Kirkcaldy along the B925 lies Auchtertool, formerly on the lands held by the Bishops of Dunkeld and later by Sir James Kirkcaldy of Grange, Lord High Treasurer to James V, who built Hallyards mansion. It is a hilly hamlet with unexpected views of Loch Gelly and Loch Camilla, and great rambling potential.

II. Dysart – West Wemyss – Coaltown of Wemyss – East Wemyss – Buckhaven – Methil – Leven

From Kirkcaldy harbour the A92 begins to leave the town as The Path and Nether Street. Nether originally meant 'low' and in this area once dwelt many of Kirkcaldy's poor folk. Demolition has greatly affected the eastern aspect of this part of Kirkcaldy, removing the old lino mills and replacing them in part with highrise blocks. Near the top of The Path, old Dunnikier House has been preserved as an important town house, built by John Watson in 1692. It was subsequently owned by the Oswald family of Dunnikier, and was renovated in 1891 to become a manse, and latterly a nurses' home. Kirkcaldy Civic Society gave the preserved work an Amenity Award in 1979 and the building was renamed Path House.

Below The Path, Pathhead Foreshore has been landscaped setting off its famous neighbour, Ravenscraig Castle. James II began the building of the castle in 1460 and it was completed as a dower-house for his widow Mary of Gueldres. Ravenscraig was one of the earliest examples of a Scottish castle to provide defence from and by artillery; it is constantly under attack from mindless vandals. It was ultimately exchanged for other properties with Earl William St Clair (Kirkcaldy's Sinclairtown is named after the family). In 1547 the castle was put to the torch by English raiders, and Cromwell 'knocked it about a bit' in 1651, but it remained in the Sinclair family until 1896. It was taken into state care in 1955 and is open to the public.

Sir Walter Scott immortalised Ravenscraig in his *The Lay of the Last Minstral* with the lines, from Canto Six, the 'piteous lay' of Harold:

> O listen, listen ladies gay!
> No haughy feat of arms I tell;
> Soft is the note, and sad the lay
> That mourns the lovely Rosabella . . .
> Last night the gifted Seer did view
> A wet shroud round layde gay;
> Then stay thee, Fair, in Ravensheuch:
> Why cross the gloomy firth to-day?

The lady Rosabelle St Clair of Rosslyn did attempt to cross the firth and died for her pains. To either side of the castle are flights of steps to the beach; both sets are claimed to be 'the 39 steps' of John Buchan's novel of the same name published in 1914.

Ravenscraig Park, with its nature trail and beehive doocot, next door to the castle, was once a part of Dysart House (1726), the policies of which were gifted to Kirkcaldy by Sir Michael Nairn; for many years the house has been a Carmelite Monastery, a community of nuns. The term 'Monastery' in this case comes from the Latin *moniales,* for contemplative nuns who made what is called a Solemn Confession, compared with the Simple Confession of convents. In 1931 the Carmelite nuns took over Dysart House which was once the hunting lodge of the Earl of Rosslyn. The Rosslyn family lived in the house until 1896 when it was sold to Sir Michael Baker Nairn. Today the enclosed order of nuns, under their Reverend Mother Prioress, have dedicated their lives to praying for the needs of the world and earn their living making altar bread hosts for the eucharist in catholic and episcopalian churches. Dysart House was linked to the policies of Ravenscraig Park by a now demolished bridge over Hot Pot Wynd.

Dysart lies alongside that part of the Fife Tourist Route (A955) which runs from Inverkeithing to the East Neuk. Within the burgh boundaries of Kirkcaldy since 1930, Dysart retains its own identity. It was long known as a linen and a mining town and place where nails were made from no less than one hundred local smithies in the 18th century. The harbour was formerly a busy port for tall ships bringing wine, pantiles, pipes and general cargoes from the Netherlands and taking away coal, salt, beer and fish; now it is a haven for small boats to live up to its old nickname of 'Little Holland'. Smugglers too knew the wynds and entries like the back of their hands and they hid their contraband all over the burgh. One piece of local partisan doggerel remembers the old trades:

Dysart for coal and saut,
Pathhead for meal and maut,
Kirkcaldy for lasses braw,
Kinghorn for breaking the law.

Those interested in architecture which has been given awards for imaginative renovation should make their way down Hot Pot Wynd – which recalls the fiery pans for salt evaporation – to Pan Ha', the ancient name for this old area of Dysart. Also taking their names from the ancient salt pans nearby, the immaculate row of white 17th-century fisher houses at Pan Ha' is now part of the National Trust for Scotland's 'Little House Improvement Scheme' which restored the block and added fine new houses.

Here too, is to be found the Bay House Inn with the lintel proclaiming 'My Hoip is in the Lord 1583' (formerly a town house of the Sinclairs), the 'Tide Waiter's' house of 1750 and the 'Salmon Fishers' Bothy' – a bothy is a Scots word to denote a workman's accommodation and the name is said to be a corruption of 'Salmon House' which had a plaster relief of a salmon in an upper room. At the junction of Cross Street and East Quality Street stands 'The Tower' of 1589, restored in 1965.

In the burgh, which was 'royal' from 1587, the Hie Gait was one of the original lanes to the shore, and in the Gait stands 'The Anchorage', a large house with a lintel dated 1582; this was the 'Harbour House' of Anna Buchan's (O. Douglas) novel *The Day of Small Things*.

Close by the harbour stands St Serf's tower, beside the ruins of the 12th-century church dedicated to the saint. The tower remains as possibly the finest example in Scotland of a battlemented church tower. In the nearby grounds of the Carmelite Monastery is the anchorite cave (not open to the public) from which St Serf is said to have sallied forth to Christianise the heathen Scots. From Serf's retreat – or *deserta* – came the burgh's name. The present church of Dysart was built in 1874, having been established as a church in 1843. In the centre of Dysart the Townhall and the much altered Tolbooth (1567-1617) are of typically Scottish design; the latter has a fine ashlar bell-chamber with ogival roof. It was used as a prison up to the 1840s.

Perhaps Dysart's most famous son was John McDouall Stuart (1815-66) who in 1861-62 was the first man to cross Australia, from the southern coast to the north, through the central desert. The National Trust for Scotland have restored the 17th-century birthplace in Rectory Lane where Stuart was born, and incorporated in it is a museum with displays describing the explorer's life, his emigration in 1838, the hardships of his travels and the aborigines and wildlife of Australia.

From Dysart the A955 makes its way north and breaks away from the shore. To the left is Frances Colliery and the Fife Police Headquarters; the Fife Constabulary dates from 1840. At the junction with the road to West Wemyss is the octagonal Bowhouse Toll, built in 1800 (rebuilt in 1906) on the old turnpike road.

The A955 skirts the castle and estate of Wemyss, belonging to the ancient Scottish family of the same name. The family and three villages take their names from the numerous large *weems*, or caves, along the coastline; some of the caves still exhibit a variety of inscriptions from the prehistoric double disc symbols to the graffiti of unfolding ages. The caves were often used as hideaways for smugglers, outlaws and gypsies, and many have names – like King's cave, where James IV is deemed to have settled a dispute amongst a band of his robber subjects during one of his incognito journeys through Fife. The caves have suffered from an incredible civic and public neglect over the years and have been repeatedly vandalised; now a Save the Wemyss Ancient Caves Society has been launched to give them some sort of care and protection.

Here too in 1610 George Hay built Scotland's first glassmaking 'factory'. Wemyss, incidentally, lends its name to that kind of pottery made in or near Kirkcaldy. Items of pottery were made by several factories including Methven & Sons of Kirkcaldy and the Fife Pottery, Gallatown; one of the characteristics of Wemyss ware was its lavish floral decorations on toilet sets, mugs, vases and so on.

The village of West Wemyss winds its way down to the shore of the Forth, and although it offers a maritime appearance, its people long depended upon the coal industry. The village grew up around Wemyss Castle and is now a conservation area. The local folk once referred to the 16th-century port and village of West Wemyss as the 'Haven Town of Wemyss', and were proud of its status as a burgh of barony, granted by James IV in 1511. West Wemyss's Tolbooth is of the 18th century, replacing the building erected 'for the cribbing of vice and service to crown' by David, 4th Earl of Wemyss (1678-1720). The old Miners' Institute (1927) is now the Belhaven Hotel (1979).

The earliest part of Wemyss Castle dates from the 14th century, but it has been added to and altered many times and is still the home of the Wemyss family. It was at the old castle of Wemyss that Mary, Queen of Scots, met Lord Darnley, soon to be her husband, in 1566. St Adrian's church below the castle along the shore was built by the Wemyss family in 1895 and it contains a rare example of a modern altar mural (1979). At West Wemyss is the southern outlet of Lochhead Tunnel which was used to transport coal (via a pulley system) to Coaltown of Wemyss and thence to Methil Dock. To the west of the village, past the tunnel's sealed entrance, lies the remains of St Mary's Chapel, a pre-Reformation church now the burial place of the Wemyss family.

Coaltown of Wemyss is bisected by the A955 and takes its name from the old mining activity at the Bell pits. Originally it was two villages, Easter and Wester, but when the miners' distinctive cottages were expanded by the Wemyss Coal Co in 1860, the two villages were amalgamated as 'a model mining village'. The village also had a public house of the Gothenburg system (see page 42), now known as the Earl David Hotel (1911). The 'rounded houses' are an interesting feature of the village.

The Wemyss School of Needlework, set by the A955, was first established in 1877 at Wemyss Castle by Lady Dorothy Wemyss, and was opened in its present building in 1880; the school began as a charity and now repairs old tapestries and undertakes orders for embroidery.

East Wemyss was once called 'Castleton' because of its nearness to Macduff Castle. This was the original home of the Wemyss family before they built Wemyss Castle in the 14th century. It is thought that Macduff Castle was the home of Macduff, Thane of Fife, from whom the Erskines of Wemyss claim descent. The term 'thane' incidentally comes from the old English *thegrian,* 'to serve'. East Wemyss is the home of the Wemyss Environmental Education Centre, an imaginative venture set up in 1977. The aim of the centre is to develop an interest in the environment and a concern for conservation and care; open daily; it has a large amount of interpretive material on local industry, people, history, flora and fauna.

The church of St Mary's-by-the-Sea at East Wemyss dates from the 12th century, but it was closed for worship in 1976 and is now a private house, although its graveyard is open to public access. The village once relied on the Michael Pit for its major employment; opened in 1898 by the Wemyss Coal Co, the pit closed in 1967.

There's a local tradition that the earliest inhabitants of Buckhaven were Dutch whose ship was stranded here in the 16th century. It is more likely, though, that Scandinavian settlers set up a fishing community here as early as the 9th century. The development of the coal industry swept away the last vestiges of the fishing port which Daniel Defoe visited during his tour in 1723, and Buckhaven – pronounced 'Buckhyne' by the old folk – is, with Methil, the industrial core of Levenmouth.

Weaving flourished in Buckhaven in the 17th and 18th centuries to form a community distinct from the fisherfolk, and for a long time intermarriage between the two was frowned upon. As fishing declined, so did Buckhaven's harbour; it is gone now and its lifeboat was sold in 1932. But Buckhaven witnessed the launch in 1985 of the locally-built 13-foot clinker-built boat the *Sea King*. It was named after the *Sea King* which in 1870 brought, stone by stone, the old episcopal church of

1825 which had stood in North Street, St Andrews. The Free Church congregation had bought the church for £130 and re-erected it next to the present parish church of St David's (1869), at the corner of Church Street and Lawrence Street; old St Andrew's has now become a theatre and community centre.

Buckhaven was once a popular holiday resort in the days before mining waste polluted the beach. Mining was re-introduced to Buckhaven in 1864 by Bowman & Co and the Old Denbeath mine was sunk in the 1870s. Between Buckhaven and Methil was the small village of Links of Buckhaven and in time the whole village was covered with pit waste and the houses vanished. Buckhaven was known too for its 'Miner Fishermen' – they worked in the pits in the winter and went to sea in the summer. The shoreline hereabouts is now overshadowed by the Redpath de Groot Caledonian oil platform construction yard, which dates from 1978, and was built on the site of the Wellesley Colliery (closed in 1967).

The town of Buckhaven is remembered in the old rhyme:

> The canty carles of Dysart,
> The merry lads of Buckhaven,
> The saucy limmers o'Largo, *cheeky women*
> The bonnie lasses of Leven.

Methil, a free burgh of barony by 1665, became the seaport of the three sister towns, edging into prominence after land reclamation projects made Leven unsuitable for large vessels. Methil rose to prominence, too, through the enterprise of the Wemyss family whose coal and salt interests led to dock development, particularly during 1872-75 when the redoubtable Mrs Wemyss (on behalf of her son Randolph Gordon Erskine Wemyss, then a minor) sponsored a wet dock. Randolph Wemyss carried on his mother's work until by 1900 Methil's dock was exporting 1,682,000 tons of Fife coal.

Between Methil and Leven lay the once separate fishing and salt panning community of Innerleven, which, like Kirkland, Aberhill, Denbeath and Methilhill had long enjoyed its own identity. Innerleven, from which fish was sent to the Priory of Markinch in medieval times, is perhaps the most 're-named' place in Fife, having variously been called Coldcoits,

The fine town house called Path House was built by John Watson in 1692 in what was then the village of Dunnikier. Once owned by the prominent Oswald family, the mansion was renovated in 1891 when it became a manse for the ministers of Dunnikier church. Its restoration by the Fife Health Board as a nurses' home won an Amenity Award from Kirkcaldy Civic Society in 1976.

Dubbieside and Salt-grieve.

Set in Largo Bay, at the mouth of its eponymous river, Leven once formed the busy port of *Levynsmouth* which saw the unloading of meat carcasses bought for the royal court when based at Falkland Palace. In 1602 Leven was banned from importing or exporting any goods, so great was the contraband in these parts. Today Leven, which was once blurbed by its publicity department as 'The Sun's Own Favourite Resort', seeks to be a prominent tourist location and promotes such facilities as its public park at Letham Glen (1925) and its attractive stretch of sands, rather than the sea trade of yesteryear. These days a power station dominates the mouth of the Leven, and where ships anchored in the roads of Leven in Largo Bay huge oil platforms sit to interrupt the view.

The roomy, handsome houses of Leven tell of its genteel past when it was a handloom centre and residential area, jolted into the 20th century by engineering and coal mining, the ubiquitous interests of the Wemyss Family. In modern times Shorehead's car parks and bus station were constructed on the site of the harbour, filled in in 1910; and the bridge which carries the A955 across the Leven replaced the 1826 toll bridge – the Bawbee Bridge which took its name from the 'bawbee' (a halfpenny) it cost to cross.

Formerly the Durie family held sway here as landowners and their estates passed on to the famous Scottish judge, Sir Alexander Gibson of Libberton, whose kidnap by litigants won immortality in Sir Walter Scott's tale 'Christie's Will' in *Minstrelsy of the Scottish Border*. Durie House (1762) was brought by the Christies in 1785 and is still inhabited by the same family.

Scoonie, the parish name taken by Leven's golf course, reminds of how its parish church was granted to the Culdees of Loch Leven by Tuadal, Bishop of St Andrews in the 1060s; the church became redundant when a new church was built at Leven in 1775, but the ruins of this original church on the incline by the A915 to Largo subsequently became the burial vault of the families who dwelt in Durie House.

In the centre of Leven stands the Greig Institute, now the public library and Tourist Information Office. The building was constructed in 1872 as a 'peoples' institute' and was named after one of its prominent promoters. On Scoonie Road, leading into the town, is Carberry House, presented to Leven in 1929 by Sir Robert Balfour as a memorial to his brother and to be used as municipal chambers; it is still used as the local headquarters of the Kirkcaldy District Council. Leven's old Mercat Cross – a red sandstone sundial of around 1623 – sits in the grounds of Carberry House, having been discovered in 1889 forming part of a wall near the Greig Institute.

Just outside Leven, along the B927 to Cupar, there stands the forlorn ruin of Aithernie Castle, a fitting memorial to Lady Margaret Lindsay of Edzell who lived here and reduced her family to penury with her spending.

III. Windygates – Kennoway – Milton of Balgonie – Markinch – Star – Coaltown of Balgonie

The hinterland of Fife's industrial south may be reached down the A915 along the north edge of Leven past Denbeath industrial estate and the blending, bottling and storage complex of the Distillers Co Ltd. Windygates still stands at a major road crossing which in past years was its lifeblood, but the main road to Kirkcaldy is now realigned to avoid the centre of the village.

Windygates was once bisected by the stagecoach routes between north and central Fife and the ferries on the south shore of the county. Posting was its principal industry and tolls were levied on the roads hereabouts until 1907. At the crossroads formed by the A915/A916/A911 is to be found Windygates Clock; its inscription reads 'Erected from the proceeds of Social Betterment Dairy Scheme'. The clock was set up in 1916 and recalls the time when the government of the day tried to encourage people to forswear alcohol and drink milk; it appears that excessive imbibing of alcohol was hampering the munitions production of World War I.

Cameron Hospital lies to the south of Windygates and was opened in 1911 as a fever hospital; its grounds take in the former mansion of Cameron House. The old smithy of Windygates is opposite the hospital gates. Down from the hospital and over the railway bridge stands Bridgend House (1869), once owned by the Haig family. By Cameron Bridge is the distillery which James Haig acquired from Eddington of West Wemyss in 1818. The Distillers Co Ltd took over the firm in 1877 and Guinness acquired it in 1986.

Cameron Bridge across the River Leven replaces one which tradition dated from 1532, built at the instigation of Cardinal David Beaton. Formerly, the settlement of Cameron Bridge was a place of spinners and bleachers. Balcurvie, with its mansion house of pre-1854, is now a part of Windygates, but it was once a separate entity. Across the Kennoway Burn to the north of Balcurvie is Kingsdale House which was built in the 18th century by James Stark and enlarged in 1864.

The A916 leads out of Windygates to Kennoway as Kennoway Road and passes the Pictish motte of Maiden Castle, known as Dunipace Hill, which legend assigns to Macduff, Thane of Fife.

The church lands of Kennoway, a village of weavers, belonged to the Priory of St Andrews from the middle of the 12th century, and its secular policies to the Earls of Rothes. The original village centred on the Causeway which retains some 18th-century houses. A weaver's house was usually a small one-storey dwelling roofed with red pantiles, and was the weaver's workshop as well as his living quarters; one small building had to house his loom, his wife and his family. The pre-Reformation church at Kennoway, dedicated to St Kenneth, was administered by the Augustinians of St Andrews, and the present parish church was erected in 1850; the church still owns the oldest Communion Cup (1671) in Scotland. Forbes House (c.1800) and Seton House (18th century), whose predecessors both claim to have sheltered Archbishop James Sharp on his last night on earth (see page 00), are situated in the town. Kennoway Den, with its sandstone cliffs, offers a number of interesting walks; the area was at one time the town's bleaching fields. Today, Kennoway is a dormitory town which saw modern expansion with the coming of Ayrshire miners in 1930 and 1950.

To the north of Kennoway is the estate of Montrave which in 1160 belonged to the nuns of North Berwick. The old mansion was built in 1810 and the estate was acquired by the Gilmour family in the late 1860s; the mansion house was reconstructed in 1887 and demolished in 1969. Montrave was the home of Lt Col The Rt Hon Sir John Gilmour (1876-1940) of Montrave and Lundie, who became Secretary of State for Scotland 1924-29 and Home Secretary 1932-35. His son, Brevet Col Sir John Gilmour, was succeeded in 1987 as Lord Lieutenant of Fife by The Rt. Hon. The Earl of Elgin and Kincardine.

Milton of Balgonie lies along the banks of the river Leven on the A911 from Windygates to Markinch. The village began as an agricultural community, but mining was carried on here from the 13th century until the pit closures of 1960. Formerly known for its iron (Leven Iron Co, 1802), its brickmaking and its flax mill (1806), from which 'Milton' was derived, today the village is largely a workers' dormitory for Glenrothes, Leven and Markinch. Milton House dates from 1770 and the village church was built in 1836 by the Balfour family as a Chapel of Ease to its parent St Drostan's at Markinch. The Miners' Welfare Institute (1926) is now used as a village hall.

The site of Balfour House lies across the river Leven and was the home of the Balfour family, who had owned the land here since around 1040. The estate fell to the Beaton (Bethune) family who were great royal favourites and influential at court; two scions of the family, who had close connections with Fife, were the uncle and nephew Archbishops of St Andrews, James (c. 1480-1539) and Cardinal David Beaton (c.1494-1546). In 1856 Arthur James Balfour (1848-1930), first Earl of Balfour, succeeded to the estates and the house; a Conservative MP, Balfour was Prime Minister during 1902-05. The house – claimed to be the first in Fife to have electricity fitted in 1882 – was dismantled in 1930, and the four trees planted in honour of her 'Maries' by Mary, Queen of Scots during a visit to the house, were cut down in the mid-1980s. One of the 'Maries' was Mary Bethune of Creich and Balfour.

One of the best early 15th-century towers in Scotland, Balgonie Castle – reached along the B921 from Milton of Balgonie – was built around 1400 by Sir John Sibbald. The castle's most famous owner was General Sir Alexander Leslie (c.1580-1661 – 1st Earl of Leven) who became leader of the Protestant army of the Solemn League and Covenant. The north range of the castle was constructed in his day, around 1654, and a fine garden was set out. By 1702 a three-storey east range was built and in 1716 Rob Roy McGregor captured the castle from the Hanoverian General William Cadogan. The castle was sold by the Earl of Leven in 1824 to the Balfours and they owned it until 1950 when it was purchased by the Balgonie Coal Co Ltd. Private restoration of the castle began in 1971 on its resale and today it has become a family home once more, having been bought in 1985 by the Morris family. The castle is open to the public at set times.

South-west of Milton of Balgonie, on the B921, lies Coaltown of Balgonie whose name would suggest that the original village was built to house miners working on the Balgonie estate. Divided by the railway, Coaltown of Balgonie is a mixture of weavers' and mining cottages and its first church was not opened until 1908.

Once called Dalgynch, the Pictish capital of Fife, Markinch was long both an industrial centre and a watering hole for tourists, advertised as 'the garden of Scotland'. The town spread out from the parish church situated at Kirk Brae, high above Glass Street, but now it has been overtaken by its young neighbour, Glenrothes. The much-restored church is on the site of the one dedicated to St Drostan which had been gifted by the Earl of Fife to the Priory at St Andrews about 1203. The Norman tower of the church remains, but the spire was altered in 1807 and the interior was reconstructed in 1883. At the church gate is a session house into which is inserted a 13th-century foliaceous capital and a niche canopy of later date. Balbirnie church in Balbirnie Street dates from 1898 and was often referred to as 'the cathedral'; it is now used as a store. In 1877 Markinch was selected as the permanent home of the whisky blenders John Haig & Co and their premises overlook a fine railway viaduct. The square-towered Town Hall in Betson Street dates from 1897 and was the gift of James Smith, partner in Tullis & Co.

Chartered by Charles II in 1673, Markinch has hilly places of note; the sister hill to the one on which the parish church stands is Markinch Hill – with its interesting cultivation terraces suggesting medieval activity – and was presented to the town in 1919 by Edward Balfour. Next to Markinch Hill, set on the banking to the left of Stobbcross Road as it leaves Markinch for Star, is Stobb Cross, which is thought to have stood at the entrance to St Drostan's church. The monument is considered by historians to be a gyrth cross which marked the boundary of an early sanctuary area. In medieval times every consecrated church had the right of sanctuary, and often provided the only refuge from summary feudal justice until a just and proper trial could be arranged. A knoll around which Northall cemetery (reached by the road under the railway bridge) was set out in the 1840s is the last resting place of many of the Balfour family.

To the north-west of Markinch lies Balbirnie Park, another Balfour family home. Balbirnie House was first built in 1777 by John Balfour in the neo-classical style on the site of an earlier dwelling; the house was added to during 1815-19 and is now the administrative headquarters of Glenrothes District Council;

James II began building Ravenscraig Castle in 1460 as a defence against the English and pirates who harried the Firth of Forth. After his death from a cannon burst at the siege of Roxburgh, his widow, Mary of Gueldres, completed the building. In time the castle came into the ownership of the St Clair family, Earls of Orkney. Today it is maintained by the Department of the Environment and the castle is open to visitors daily via Ravenscraig Park.

Glenrothes Development Corporation acquired the property in 1969. Within Balbirnie Park is a caravan park, a golf course, a Bronze Age stone circle and the noteworthy Balbirnie Craft Centre of 1972, which offers visitors an all-the-year-round permanent showcase of crafts from stained glass to furniture.

Of all Fife's villages, the name of Star is one of the most pleasing – it derived from 'starr', a swamp. The village lies to the north-east of Balbirnie Park and was a weaving community; largely unspoilt by modern architecture, the slightly elevated village has some fine views of the Lomond Hills and offers a variety of country walks. The old schoolhouse was the home of the Scottish novelist Annie S. Swan (1859-1943); she lived in the house when her husband, Dr James Burnett Smith, was dominie.

IV. Glenrothes – Leslie – Thornton

Glenrothes has the enthusiasm and confidence associated with the young. Indeed there is an assurance to be seen clearly at Markinch station as the visitor alights for Glenrothes. There on the wall of an old engine shed, Glenrothes proclaims itself to be 'the capital of Fife'. Hoary academics and Fife bureaucrats elsewhere might dispute the claim, but Glenrothes has the verve for all that. The new town is undoubtedly the administrative centre of the Fife Region, with such headquarters buildings as those of the Fife Health Board and the South of Scotland Electricity Board, and Fife Regional Council has all its departments located in Glenrothes. The Fife Institute of Physical and Recreational Education is based here too. Throughout the town are open-air examples of modern art from clay murals to sculptures; these are mostly by town artists, the reintroduction of whom to the architectural team was pioneered in the United Kingdom by Glenrothes.

From its beginnings Glenrothes was a New Town with inherent differences. It was not a satellite of a major city; it was not an overspill for slums; and, it was not the settlement area for industry displaced by urban redevelopment. Thus it soon became a community with its own personality as it was not centred on an existing township. Glenrothes is set out on land from the old Rothes, Balfour, Balgonie and Aytoun estates and the area only had the villages of Woodside and Cadham as a focus with a scattering of farmhouses and cottages. The Glenrothes Development Corporation began its work during 1948-49 and this was the authority mainly responsible for the development of the new town which was born out of the New Towns Act of 1946.

Industry was to be centred on the new Rothes pit at Thornton which went into production in 1957; alas it closed in 1961 through various geological faults and the closure meant a new direction for the town planners. Even so the names of the old collieries in the district have been incorporated in street names remembering the mines at Cadham (1741), Thornton (1842) and Lochtyside (1845). The first new industry to open in Glenrothes was Beckman Instruments at Queensway Industrial Estate in 1958. Glenrothes was the first New Town to have its own airstrip, opened in 1964. A building programme was under way by 1950, and the first house was opened at Woodside in 1951; the first phase of the New Town, Woodside/Auchmuty, was finalised by 1960. The first church to be opened in Glenrothes was St Margaret's Church of Scotland parish church in 1954. The Glenrothes District Council was launched in 1961.

The largest single employer in the Glenrothes area is Messrs Tullis Russell & Co Ltd at their papermill situated by the River Leven. They are an amalgam of what were once two separate firms, Rothes Mill (1806) and Auchmuty Mill (1809), various amalgamations thereafter resulting in Tullis Russell (1906). Today they are still the largest privately owned paper manufacturer in Europe. Today, also, Glenrothes is a major micro-electronics centre within Scotland's 'Silicone Valley' and Tullis Russell are likely to be surpassed as employers by Hughes Microelectronics of California whose European headquarters in Glenrothes is undergoing a £25 million expansion that will bring the workforce to around 1200 by 1990.

A close neighbour of Glenrothes, across the valley of the River Leven, is Leslie, once called Fythkill, or Fettykill. The name Leslie derives from a former landowner hereabouts, the descendant of Bartholomew the Fleming from Leslie in Aberdeenshire. Leslie was a spinning and weaving community and the symbols of the trade are still to be seen carved on door lintels; but paper and plastics have contributed to Leslie's more recent industrial life.

Leslie did not develop municipally until 1865 when it became a police burgh, but it was long thought to be the location of the popular Scottish poem *Christis Kirk on the Grene*, attributed by some to James I and by others to James V. The poem refers to Leslie wappinshaw, or fair, for the town was once famous for its ebullient festivities:

> Was never in Scotland heard or seen
> Sic dancing and deray;
> Nowther at Falkland on the green,
> Nor Peblis at the play,
> As was of woers, as I ween,
> At Christ's Kirk on ane day . . .

The chapmen – the itinerant pedlars and carriers – are said to have had their headquarters at Leslie where they met on the Green for sport and recreation; new members were initiated in a ducking ceremony. Martinmas Fair was also popular at Leslie for this was the final fling for the villagers and their neighbours before the hardships of winter.

Leslie was a place of combats and bull-baiting and its Bull Stone is still situated on the Green. To this granite boulder bulls were chained to be baited by dogs. The stone is deeply grooved with chain and rope marks. Bull-baiting was popular from the 12th to the 19th centuries and was declared illegal in 1835.

Leslie House, the 'Villa de Rothes' from a title derived from estates around Elgin in Morayshire, was the centre of the Burgh of Barony by the 15th century. The house was built by Sir William Bruce for John Leslie, Duke of Rothes, Charles II's Lord High Chancellor of Scotland; the house was visited by Daniel Defoe in 1707. The house was the residence too of the Earls of Rothes and was destroyed by fire in 1763; the west wing was reconstructed in 1767. The house long displayed a dagger with which it is said one Norman Leslie, Master of Rothes, murdered Cardinal David Beaton at St Andrews in 1546. The house is now a Church of Scotland Eventide Home, having been gifted in 1953 by Sir Robert Spencer-Nairn of the Kirkcaldy lino family.

Leslie's post-Reformation church was founded in 1591 and dismantled in 1819 and a new one set up in 1820; this building forms the rear of the present church extended in 1868-9 to include a steeple. The churchyard contains the twin-gabled burial vault of the Rothes family.

To the west of Leslie (off the A911) is Strathendry House built by Robert Douglas in the early 19th century and nearby are the ruins of Strathendry Castle. Within the vicinity of Leslie too are the ruins of the 17th-century Pitcairn House. Balgeddie House was built as a family home by the Nairns of Kirkcaldy in 1936; it still retains its floors built out of ships' timbers from Inverkeithing; the house was converted into a hotel in 1969.

Glenrothes' neighbour to the south, linked by the A92, is Thornton – Thorn Town – which sprang to fame as an important railway junction and was the centre of the East Fife

St Serf's Tower rises above the ruined 12th-century church and dominates the immaculate white houses in the area of Dysart known as Pan Ha', the ancient name which recalls the days when salt panning was a major industry hereabouts. The renovated houses are part of the National Trust for Scotland's 'Little Houses' scheme which began in the 1960s. Six of the old fishermen's houses were restored and a new block of five houses was added to blend with the originals *(Fife Regional Council).*

coalfields. The massive towers for the winding gear of the disused Rothes pit are still visible for miles around. Thornton was once an important staging village with famous hostelries like the Beech Inn and Strephan's Inn; before the bypass was fully opened in 1983, Thornton was one of the worst bottlenecks in Fife. Thornton station was closed in 1969, but it won literary fame when the chief secretary for Ireland-cum-author Augustine Birrell (1850-1933) opined that Thornton's platforms were the most 'salubrious' he had ever encountered.

Thornton's parish church in the main street was erected in 1835 and contains only one gravestone set up in 1845 to Thomas Lindsay aged eleven months. The nearby Town Clock, set in its distinctive black and white turret, was the gift of Mr Waldegrave Leslie of Leslie House to mark Queen Victoria's Jubilee of 1897.

One of the avenues in Thornton celebrates the new type of flute – the flutorum – invented by an eccentric Dunfermline weaver who opened a pub in Thornton. His name was David Hatton and he had tried to win fame with the invention of the 'mouse treadmill' for winding spools of thread – the industrialists of the day were unimpressed. For many years before he died in 1851 Hatton used to exhibit the coffin in which he was to be buried, and for a penny would lie in it to entertain his clientele. Another famous resident of Thornton was James Black, the government clerk who copied out the American Declaration of Independence from Thomas Jefferson's own copy.

The A92 out of Glenrothes leads northwards to skirt the foot of the East Lomond at New Inn, an important coaching stop of past years; the inn had been built around 1800 and was demolished in 1963. To the right across the modern dual carriageway are Kirkforthar Feus with the ruined chapel of Kirkforthar and the crumbling Kirkforthar house and doocot; the house is a 17th-century edifice with 18th-century remodelling.

CHAPTER 3

Falkland and the Howe of Fife

I. The Lomond Hills

The whole of central and north west Fife is dominated by the twin volcanic peaks of the Lomond Hills which rise to almost 1750 feet at West Lomond and 1500 at East Lomond. The Lomond Hills began to form in the Carboniferous Age, some 350 million years ago, and today the heather moorland is managed for red grouse which share the hill with roe deer, foxes, chaffinches and wood pigeon; the rough grassland is tended for summer grazing. The six-mile long quartz dolerite hills, rising above a moorland saddle, are best seen from the Howe of Fife, that verdant plain lying to the north of the hills. A 'howe' incidentally is a hollow, or a low-lying piece of ground, and the hills afford spectacular views of the whole county. From the east the hills rise ruggedly and steeply towards the north, but gradually and smoothly to the south. In the 18th century lead was worked and silver extracted on the East Lomond in the region of Hangingmyre Farm. A rumour of gold being found on West Lomond started a 'gold rush' in 1852. There are still relics of the old sandstone quarries and limekilns, and a keen eye can trace the medieval rig and plough marks.

East Lomond is approached with ease up the mettled road off the A912 Falkland/New Inn road and offers parking and picnic areas. Some 20 miles of footpaths offer dozens of walks across the two Lomonds, and West Lomond has a convenient picnic/parking area at Craigmead; the latter is reached from Leslie (A911) via Pitkevy, or from Falkland through the hills. Hereabouts is an area of seven reservoirs – Harperleas, Ballo, Drumain, Holl, Balgillie, Arnot and Coul – the haunts of tufted duck, wigeon, grebes, sandpipers, redshanks and swans.

Set in the Lomond Hills section of the Fife Regional Park are two interesting forts dating from the late 1st millennium BC to the early 1st millennium AD. East Lomond's Bronze Age cairn is reached from the picnic area by the relay station, and the West Lomond Fort – known as Maiden Castle – is reached from Craigmead carpark. Around 1920 a slab bearing the Pictish figure of a bull was discovered at the south side of East Lomond Fort. Two stones feature in Lomond myth; at the foot of the West Lomond, 'Bonnet Rock' is said to cover a Pictish chieftain and was the pulpit of many a Convenanting conventicle. The 'Maiden Bower' rock nearby was a lover's trysting place long thought to be the tombstone of a jilted local girl.

II. Gateside – Strathmiglo – Falkland – Freuchie – Kingskettle – Pitlessie – Springfield – Ladybank – Bow of Fife – Letham – Monimail – Collessie – Auchtermuchty

The Howe of Fife may be enjoyed as a circular tour with Falkland and the Lomond hills as a treat along the way. The tour may start from the A91 junction with the M90 motorway, north of Milnathort, or from the Cupar direction; it matters not, for this part of Fife offers particular delights along any route. So let us enter this part of Fife via Gateside – once called Edenside – along the A91.

Within the Old Village, off the main road, is an 18th-century smithy and adjoining houses, but the settlement is very much older, having been the site of the chapel of St Mary of Dungaitside belonging to the monks of Balmerino Abbey. The Church of Edenshead, on the main road, dates from 1826. On the eastern edge of the village, just off the A91, down by the river Eden are the Gateside Mills, recalling how once the village was noted for its bobbin and shuttle mills, the suppliers of weaving factories all over the world. The bridge of Eden dates back from the 19th century and both Edenshead House and Gateside House go back to the 18th century, though the former was renovated in 1900.

The modern road follows the line of the old Ladybank-Kinross railway, and opposite the tourist car park stands the three-storied ruined 16th-century Corston Tower; this occupies the site of a 15th-century residence built by the prominent

The High Street, Strathmiglo, *circa* 1910, overshadowed by the steeple of the square town house. Standing 70ft high with its open balustrade and octagonal spire, the tower is a fine piece of Scottish burgh architecture. The townsfolk built their tower out of stone from Sir William Scott of Balwearie's ruined Strathmiglo Castle in 1734. The tower bears the arms of the Balfours of Burleigh, and the base was once Strathmiglo's lock-up *(Peter Adamson)*.

denizen of James II's court, John Ramsay. Opposite the junction with the road to Strathmiglo is Pitlour estate with its house of 1784, stables, icehouse and 19th-century lodges. Strathmiglo was bypassed in 1969.

The old barony burgh of Strathmiglo (Eglismartin – 'the church of St Martin) has two distinct 15th-century districts, Kirklands and Templelands, recalling that the lands were once divided between the medieval collegiate church and pedagogy and the Knights Templar and thereafter the Knights Hospitallers. Of the former it is said that they were introduced into Scotland by David I around 1128. The Templars, or Poor Knights of Christ and of the Temple of Solomon, were a religious order founded around 1120 in Jerusalem by a group of French knights. They were sworn to protect the pilgrim routes to the Holy Land, as were the knights of the Order of the Hospital of St John of Jerusalem, who were landlords in Strathmiglo until the 19th century. The Templars and the Hospitallers were landowners in Fife rather than residents. Today Strathmiglo is still divided in two by the river Eden which separates the more modern dwellings from the ancient heart.

Of the buildings within Strathmiglo the tolbooth with its open balustrade and octagonal spire in the High Street takes pride of place. Its stone came from Strathmiglo Castle, the mansion house of Sir William Scott of Balwearie, a courtier of James V; the house had been refurbished to impress James V who, in the event, was underwhelmed, and the mansion fell in ruins by 1734. The arms on the tolbooth tower are of later landowners hereabouts, the Balfours of Burleigh. The village, once the home of prominent merchants who supplied Falkland Palace, has an interesting set of 18th-19th century houses and taverns. One of the most unusual of Scotland's rights of way leads through Strathmiglo Inn: a sign above the passage door indicates the twenty-four hour right of access to Back Dykes. By the picnic area is the California; the word means spring of cold water and the well has gushed forth here for countless generations. Although agriculture and supplying back-up services to Falkland Palace were once the staple bread-winning occupations of Strathmiglo, Skene Street still has cottages with the heavy ceiling beams once associated with the construction

The road leading to the West Port, Falkland, photographed 16 October 1950, before the royal burgh's extensive restoration. The house with the outside stairs on the left is the Reading Room, an 18th-century house imaginatively restored today to house an electricity sub-station. The sign points to the Stag Inn, down Mill Wynd, with its lintel of 1680. *(D.C. Thomson & Co Ltd).*

of handlooms. A.T. Hogg (1858-1927) was once described as the 'man who made Strathmiglo famous'; he pioneered the selling of boots by post and his 'Fife Boots' won international fame; the firm he founded is still located in the village.

Strathmiglo manse originated in 1785 and the church with its bellcote dates from 1784, although there was a pre-Reformation church in the village dedicated to St Martin, Bishop of Tours. Once Strathmiglo's November Fair to celebrate the Feast of St Martin was famous throughout Scotland, but James II caused it to be moved to Cupar in 1437. The pre-Reformation church was sited in the present burying ground in which is set the much weathered but noteworthy Moray Monument of 1646, and within the 18th-century church are two memorial windows to the Middleton brothers who all perished in World War I. South of Strathmiglo are East and West Cash Feus with 18th-19th century dwellings and weavers' cottages; the feus once belonged to the Marquess of Bute, the renovator of Falkland Palace.

The village of Strathmiglo is linked to Falkland, the capital of the ancient Stewartry of Fife, by way of the A912, which forms New Road and the Pleasance within Falkland village. 'A pretty little Town . . . a stately Palace' is how the Dutch engraver, John Slezer, described the weaving village of Falkland which has retained the atmosphere that he saw in the 17th century. Falkland was made a Royal Burgh in 1458 by James II and its buildings reflect the personalities of the courtiers and tradesmen who used to live in the medieval burgh; all of which architecture is preserved through conservation orders. Falkland's modern industry is centured on tourism and a 'factory', a former linen works now making paper and plastic bags.

From the A912 the visitor enters Falkland's East Port and on the left, opposite the Palace, stands Moncrieff House. A two-storied 17th-century building thatched with Tay reeds, Moncrieff House has a marriage lintel dated 1610 and a signed plaque of the same date for Nicoll Moncrief, King's Averiman, a servitor in charge of the Royal Stables of James VI. The Hunting Lodge Hotel (1607) next door also has carved and painted stones. Across Back Wynd is the steepled Georgian Town House of 1801 with the arms of the burgh showing a stag sitting under an oak. The Town House, now a visitor centre for the National Trust for Scotland, fronts the old market square in the centre of which is the Bruce Fountain (1856) with the arms of the burgh and those of the Keeper of the Palace who provided the fountain and the Gothic church of 1849; the manse of 1807 is in Chapel Yard. Next to the church is the memorial statue to the fountain and church benefactor, one Onesiphorus Tyndall-Bruce who also built the House of Falkland (1839-44). Around the square too are the 18th-century white-harled St Andrews House and Key House (1713), with its Angus roof slabs, once the Palace Inn.

Next to the Town House, is the Covenanter Hotel (1771) whose name related to the house in the south-west corner of the square, the birthplace of schoolmaster Richard Cameron

An Austin 7 car nestles under the boundary wall of Falkland Palace in the medieval royal burgh's High Street, in this photograph of 8 September 1936. Open to the public at set times, Falkland Palace is a picturesque royal dwelling of Renaissance style, dating from 1501-41. It was the favourite seat of James V, who died here in 1542, and of his daughter Mary, Queen of Scots. The Royal Tennis Court is still played on, and the gardens are a delightful bonus for visitors *(D.C. Thomson & Co Ltd)*.

(1648-80), the famous Covenanter – he is associated with the naming of the Cameronian Regiment in 1689. Cross Wynd is lined by single-storied cottages, interrupted only by cobbled Parliament Square. Houses of varying dates and worthy of exploration are to be found in Mill Wynd, Castle Street, and Back Wynd. Down Mill Wynd is the Stag Inn of 1680. The 18th-century Reading room sub-station was restored by the South of Scotland Electricity Board in 1960 and was once two houses, of which one was home for a family of 13! Around 1850 the lower house was used as a reading room, in which a local stonemason, Thomas Drysdale, read newspapers, tracts, pamphlets and books to the illiterate inhabitants of the burgh. Brunton House (1712), Brunton Street, was the home of the Simsons of Brunton, hereditary Royal Falconers.

A monument worthy of mention on Black Hill is the Bruce Monument (1855) set up to the memory of the burgh benefactor Onesiphorus Tyndall-Bruce, who did much to make work for the local unemployed and fed the needy.

An hour should be allocated to savour Falkland Palace, the royal hunting lodge which developed out of the castle built by the family of Macduff, Thane of Fife.

In the 14th century, the castle passed to the Stewarts and by 1458 it was being referred to as 'a palace'; its undoubted heyday was during the 15th and 16th centuries. The last royal resident of the Palace was Charles II in 1650, who was in Scotland for his coronation, and the Palace fell into a state of disrepair after the Jacobite rising of 1715. Yet, the Palace retained its Hereditary Keeper, and it was the most flamboyantly named Keeper, Onesiphorus Tyndall-Bruce, who was advised by Sir Walter Scott to restore the Palace as a 'romantic ruin'. In 1887 John Crichton Stuart, 3rd Marquess of Bute, acquired the Keepership from the Tyndall-Bruces and undertook a massive programme of restoration. Today the palace is still in the ownership of the monarch and the Crichton Stuarts are still keepers, with the National Trust for Scotland as Deputy Keepers since 1952.

These days the visitor enters the Palace by way of the Gatehouse which dates from 1541 and bears the refurbished coats of arms of the Royal Lyon of Scotland, the Lyon of the Earls of Fife and the Arms of Stuart of Bute. Thence, the visitor enters the South Range with its vaulted cellars and Tapestry Gallery and the most outstanding feature of all, the Chapel Royal, begun by James IV. The Crichton Stuarts are Roman Catholics and the chapel is used regularly for Holy Mass. In the antechamber of the chapel are the colours of the Scots Guards who have had an association with the Palace since Charles II 'christened' the regiment here in 1650. Part of the private quarters of the Keepers of the Palace may be seen in the Drawing Room and the Old Library. The East Range dates from the days of James IV and contains the royal apartments.

Across the roofless second floor of the East range is the King's Bed Chamber which was rebuilt by the 3rd Marquess; here James V died in 1542. That year James's army had been defeated by Henry VIII's forces at Solway Moss, a disaster to

Freuchie Cricket Club was founded in 1908, and in 1985 their team won the National Village Championship at Lords, defeating the team from the Surrey village of Rowledge. The winning team here photographed at Lords were:
Back Row: Niven McNaughton; Stewart Irvine; Peter Hepplewhite; George Wilson; David Cowan; Mark Wilkie; Brian Christie; Fraser Irvine.
Front Row: George Crichton; Alan Duncan; David Christie (Captain); Andy Crichton; Terrence Trewartha *(D.C. Thomson & Co Ltd).*

add to his mourning the death of his two infant sons in 1541. At Falkland James heard that his wife, Marie de Guise-Lorraine, had given birth to a daughter at Linlithgow Palace, West Lothian, on the Feast of the Immaculate Conception of the Virgin Mary, 8 December 1542. He declared the event the worst of his doom laden life. And, at six days old, Mary became Queen of Scotland, for James turned his face to the wall of his chamber in Falkland Palace and as he died muttered sourly about the fate of his family, the Stewarts. 'The Devil go with it,' he said. 'It came with a lass and it will go with a lass.' In this prognostication James was as premature as his daughter. Although the house of Stewart had been founded by Marjorie Bruce – daughter of Robert I, the Bruce – when she married Walter Stewart in 1315, their house was to be royal for years to come . . . yet the line did come to an end in 1714 at the death of Queen Anne.

The foundations of the North Range of the Palace and the Round Tower of the original Macduff fortress can be seen in the gardens replanted as a modern formal garden. Beyond is the 1539 Royal Tennis Court, built only eight years after Henry VIII's tennis court at Hampton Court.

The B936 out of Falkland links Newton of Falkland with the village of Freuchie. Newton had a long association with brewing and malting and the maltings, with their pagoda-like outlets on the roofs, are a reminder of the old trade. There are still a few 18th-century weavers' cottages in the hamlet. Freuchie also had a linen factory, but this is now used for the commercial cultivation of mushrooms. The Albert Tavern is 18th century, as are many of the village cottages; the church dates from 1875. There is local tradition that Freuchie was the place where French masons dwelt who worked on Falkland Palace in the 16th century and that the village served as a place of exile for disgraced courtiers from Falkland; modern-day Freuchie folk recall that within living memory people in this part of Fife used such dismissive phrases as: 'Awa' tae Freuchie, whaur the Froggies live'.

Kingskettle lies to the north-east of Freuchie and takes its name from *catel,* a battle, of which one was fought, tradition has it, between the Scots and Danes near the modern village. There is a pleasant local story that the battle gave Scotland its emblem of the thistle; the tale recounts that the Scots were roused from their slumbers when one of the invading Danes trod on a thistle and let out a yell! In truth, however, the thistle head did not make its appearance as a Scottish emblem until the minting of the groats of James III in 1471. The name Kingskettle first appears in a charter of 1541, by which time the lands hereabouts were Crown property within the hunting forest of Falkland.

Known locally as Kettle, the old parish takes in the villages of Kettlebridge, 18th-century Balmalcolm, Coaltown of Burnturk and Muirhead, anciently known as Lathrisk. Although there are Iron Age hill forts in the vicinity, and Bronze Age relics have been found nearby, the earliest written record of Kingskettle is the grant of lands by Malcolm IV to Duncan, Earl of Fife, in 1166. Most of the folk of Kettle formerly earned their living from the linen industry, producing material

Fernie Castle, Monimail, some four miles west of Cupar, belonged to Duncan, 13th Earl of Fife, in 1353. In 1680 the Balfours of Burleigh became the owners and their descendants held tenure until 1965. The duties of the Constable of Cupar and Forester of Falkland were associated with the Old Barony of Fernie for centuries. Today the L-plan castle, with its 16th-century fortalice and rare circular tower, is a luxury hotel *(Peter Adamson).*

for shirts and window blinds. The first power loom was opened at Kingskettle in 1864 and the last one was dismantled in 1929. Coal and lime working took place at Burnturk and Pitlessie respectively.

There is still a certain air of ease in Kettle, a comfort stop on the old turnpike road from Newport to Pettycur, and the village still nestles by the railway opened in 1847 by the North British Railway Co to link Perth and Edinburgh. In its sheltered spot in the glaciated valley of the Howe of Fife, the village retains its neat stone villas and cottages, mostly of the 18th century set around the nucleus of the elegant Gothic church of 1832 which replaced the older church of St Ethernaseus, circa 1636, which itself succeeded the church dedicated by Bishop de Bernham in 1243. The former manse dates from 1792. The earliest parish church is said to have been that of Lathrisk dating from the 14th century, now thought to be a part of Lathrisk House of 1710-80; there are sites of pre-Reformation chapels too at Clatto and Chapel-Kater. Near Kettlebridge once stood Bankton House, the long-vanished home of James Russell, one of the murderers of Archbishop James Sharp in 1679.

Along the A92 from Kettlebridge, through Balmalcolm – 'Malcolm's Town' – lies Pitlessie, the only village in the old parish of Cults, rich in arable farming land and mixed tree plantations. Pitlessie grew as a rural community with employment not only on the big estates nearby but at 19th-century Priestfield Maltings and the lime works at the mill above the village. Etymologists believe that Cults derived from the Gaelic *quylt,* a 'resting place'. Certainly the sandstone Cults Kirk with its small early 19th-century Session House and manse of 1796, was a place of rest and spiritual refreshment from its construction in 1793 during the ministry of the Rev David Wilkie. The church incidentally does not lie within Pitlessie, but off the A92 beyond Pitlessie at Kirkton.

The Rev Wilkie's son, also David, was born at the adjoining manse on the 18 November 1785. Young David's mother was the daughter of a Pitlessie miller and he attended the parish schools of Pitlessie and Kettle and thereafter the academy of Cupar. In 1799 he began to study art at the Trustees' Academy at Edinburgh. At the age of nineteen in 1804, he returned to the manse and began work on his first famous picture, 'Pitlessie Fair', (now in the National Gallery for Scotland) which contains no less than one hundred and forty faces, many of which he sketched while attending services in the parish church; indeed the picture contains a self-portrait and depictions of his father, sisters and brothers. In Wilkie's time there were two fairs held at Pitlessie, in May and October, for the sale of cattle, and it is thought that the May fair inspired Wilkie. The site of the fairs was in the middle of Pitlessie near to the house called 'Burnbrae' (once a public house). Many of young Wilkie's early drawings were to be found on the walls of the manse attic, but they were destroyed by fire in 1926. Another of Wilkie's famous pictures, 'The Village Politicians', also had its origins in Cults. In time David Wilkie won fame as a portrait painter and

Collessie village, with its fine views over a wide level stretch of the fertile Howe of Fife, once overlooked Rossie Loch and the large peat marches dug by the monks of the Abbey of Lindores, who were the superiors of the parish church re-dedicated by Bishop de Bernham in 1243; the present church dates from 1839. The woods and forests of the parish were once the hunting grounds of the Bishops of St Andrews.

in 1823 he succeeded Sir Henry Raeburn as the King's Limner (painter) in Scotland; when Sir Thomas Lawrence died in 1830 Wilkie was selected as Painter-in-Ordinary to His Majesty; Wilkie was knighted in 1836. He was travelling home from the Near East in 1841 when he died aboard ship and was buried at sea. His memorial is set by the pulpit in Cults church.

Opposite Clatto Hill, to the south of Pitlessie, is Devon Wood and the place called Torloisk; it takes its name from *tor* and *Loisgthe,* to mean 'hill of the burning', an undoubted Pictish association with the feasts of Beltane and Samhuinn, the two divisions of the Celtic year, in May and November. At these times the arrival of summer and winter were marked with bonfires. The fires of Torloisk were probably a hilltop link with the Perthshire mountains of Ben Ledi, Schiehallion and Ben More. Always a wild place of woods, heathery slopes and marshes – the reservoirs of Clatto, Carriston and Donald Rose nearby having drained the area – the landscape of Devon was rich in fauna and was a popular area for the royal hunt from Falkland. Over the hills of Kirkforthar they would race to Devon Common with its links with the *Damnonii* tribe of Roman times, to Kilmux Wood, pausing for refreshments at Mildeans and Black Tankard. These wild hills were the haunts too of the Setons who issued regulary to persecute their neighbours from their now-vanished stronghold of Clatto castle. The old gibbet tree of Clatto was still to be seen until it fell in a gale in 1927; thereafter the gibbet irons (in which the miscreant's body was hung) were long displayed at Clatto farm.

Kingskettle and Pitlessie's largest neighbour to the north is Ladybank. Known prior to the 12th century as Moss of Monegae, Ladybank was used as a peat-cutting area by the monks of Lindores Abbey, who called it 'Our Lady Bog'. Prior to the construction of burns and drainage like the great Rossie Drain from the mid-18th century, the area was very marshy with a loch. Lady's Bog was changed to Ladybank when the railway station was being planned; today the name Monkstown, a district alongside the B938 and the only part of Ladybank to predate the railway construction of the 1850s, is the sole memory of the holy brothers of Lindores.

Recalling the ancient forestlands here, almost a mile west of Ladybank is the Forestry Commission's Edensmuir Picnic Place with walks through the open woods of pine, spruce and silver birch, the haunt of chaffinch and goldcrest.

The North British Railway Co's (later LNER) junction for Perth and Kinross gave Ladybank a great boost, but because the town came into existence as a consequence of the railway it has no buildings of great age. The town was made a burgh in 1878 and was noted for its linen and maltings; Ladybank Maltings were demolished in 1986. The town's Free Church was built in 1876 and its parish church was erected in 1882. Annsmuir was formerly a training area for the local regiment, the Fife and Forfar Yeomanry. When the British Open Golf Championships is being played at St Andrews, Ladybank's fine golf course is used as a qualifying course.

Jimmy Shand, MBE, and his wife Ann proudly display the gold record presented to the famous self-taught accordionist in 1983 to celebrate his 50 years in the recording business. In 1988 Jimmy Shand, Auchtermuchty's grand old man of music, celebrated his 80th birthday. In his heyday his millions of fans worldwide claimed that listening to his toe-tapping music cured rheumatism and other ills *(D.C. Thomson & Co Ltd).*

In Ladybank's Masonic Hall – by the railway bridge and opposite the obelisk gates into Ramornie estate – H.H. Asquith, Liberal Prime Minister during 1908-16, and MP for East Fife, made many of his great speeches. The area was known for its political hecklers at election times. The word 'heckler', incidentally, comes from the vocabulary of the flax weavers and refers to the combing of the flax fibres. A plaque set by the main door of the 1890 Masonic Hall commemorates the 50th anniversary of Asquith's entrance into parliament and his adoption as Liberal candidate on 26 June 1886.

The village of Springfield is set a mile or so back from the

A92 Pitlessie-Cupar road, and retains the smallest railway station in Fife that is still open, although unmanned (the station house of 1847 is now private property). Local tradition has it that nearby Stratheden was a landlocked lake fed by numerous springs from which the village obtained its name; and in the 16th-17th centuries there was peat-cutting in the area. Because of the nature of the ground Springfield never had its own graveyard.

Down the ages Springfield has sported brick and tile works, jute and flax mills, quarries, sandpits and corn mills. Lack of industry caused Springfield's young folk to look elsewhere for work and the township of Waverley, South Dakota, USA was founded by emigrants from Springfield. Springfield's church was built in 1861 and the church clock was set up in 1878. Around the 1850s the village had its own racecourse which is now the factory area of Scot's Porage Oats. To the north of the village lies Stratheden Hospital on the site of the land known as the Retreat where Mary Queen of Scots' mother, Marie de Guise-Lorraine's army encamped during the troubles of 1559. The hospital at Stratheden was built around 1850 as a home for the mentally insane, but today few wards are locked.

The largest house in the area is Crawford Priory, set within its own wooded estate which once sported a deer park. It was built in 1813 by Lady Mary Lindsay Crawford, sister of George, 13th Earl of Crawford, on the site of a lodge built in 1758 by Lady Mary's father, Viscount Garnock. The style of the house is Gothic, with castle-monastic overtones which reflected Lady Mary's interest in things medieval. The estate passed to the Earl of Glasgow in 1833 and he made alterations and improvements in 1871, and his son-in-law, Lord Cochrane of Cults, lived regularly at the Priory until his death in 1951. The Cochrane family still live on the estate in modern homes, but the Priory is falling into disrepair.

The eccentric builder of the Priory, Lady Mary, died in 1833 and was buried at Walton Hill (to the south-east of the Priory) in the isolated mausoleum in the form of a Roman Temple, built by the 12th Earl of Glasgow in 1758. Lady Mary's obsession with animal welfare caused her to set up an elaborate gravestone near the Priory stables to her pet deer.

From Springfield, the A91 from Cupar may be joined

opposite Over Rankeillour House (c.1820) built by John Hope, 4th Earl of Hopetoun who died in 1823. His memorial on The Mount, to the north-east of Over Rankeillour, dominates the area; according to the inscription on the monument it was 'erected by the inhabitants of Fife' in 1827. The A91 leads to Bow of Fife, with its red-spired church of 1843, enlarged in 1898, and from here the minor road may be taken to the right to explore Letham, Monimail and Collessie.

All three villages have a distinct character of their own and were all self-sufficient within living memory. Letham, nestling at the foot of Letham hill, retains its village green and has interesting 18th and 19th-century houses in The Square, Parliament Square, and The Row, a string of red-pantiled weavers' cottages. A modern dormitory village, Letham sports a bakehouse of 1691 and a profusion of 17th and 18th-century doocots.

On the A914 to Dundee, and just north-east of Letham, stands Fernie Castle, which incorporates the old 16th-century tower of Fernie which itself may have been on the site of a keep belonging to Macduff, Earl of Fife. With the barony of Fernie went the titles of Forester of Falkland and Constable of Cupar. Fernie Castle fell to the Balfour family of Mountquhanie around the 15th century and was held by a cadet branch of the Balfours up to 1965, after which it became a luxury hotel. The castle is constructed on an L-plan but has been much altered, although its 16th century fortalice is discernible with its slit windows and watchtower. The stables and icehouse date from the 1820s. Fernie Castle's neighbour, the old estate of Cunnoquhie, sports an 19th-century house.

North-east of Fernie, under Mount Hill, is the place called The Mount, associated with Sir David Lindsay (c.1486-1555), poet and Lyon King of Arms. Sir David was born in Monimail parish, spent much of his life here and passed his latter days in the shelter of Mount Hill in seclusion. Educated at Cupar Grammar School and St Andrews, Sir David Lindsay's poems may be described as 'tracts of the times', and perhaps his most famous is *The Satire of the Three Estates* which castigates the evils of Church, State and Society (see page 00).

Monimail remains a picturesque corner of Fife with a number of restored properties despite the decline of the old village. Deriving its name, it seems, from the Gaelic *monadh-maol,* 'the bare hill', the area was once owned by the See of St Andrews and there was an episcopal residence here from the days of Bishop William Lamberton (1298-1328), of which Monimail Tower remains as a relic. Certainly, John Hamilton, the last medieval Archbishop of St Andrews, still used it as a residence in the mid-16th century. While at Monimail, an old legend goes, the archbishop was tended by one Girolamo Cardano of Milan, an astrologer and physician, who is purported to have used water from a local well in his potions to cure the asthmatic archbishop; this mineral well was long described as 'Cardan's Well'. Monimail Tower is ascribed to Hamilton's predecessor Cardinal David Beaton and is all that remains of a larger edifice overlooking the parish graveyard in which are buried the Earls of Leven, Balfour and Melville. Monimail church was built in 1796 to replace its ruinous predecessor, and its Gothic tower dates from 1811; the church is of the T-plan and has unusual fenestrations.

Melville House at Monimail dates from 1692 and its garden houses from 1697, and all are the work of the 1st Earl of Melville. The estate continued in the Melville family until the present century and was dismantled piecemeal during 1938-50; today the house is a school for boys in care. The surrounding gardens of Melville House date from 1825 and were bought, with Monimail Tower, by the Monimail Tower Project in 1984. Excavations at the tower took place in 1987 and plans to restore it are underway by members of the Project.

Collessie was an agricultural centre with handloom weaving as a subsidiary industry some hundred years ago, but its history is longer than that, for prehistoric activity is witnessed by the Bronze Age relics discovered in the parish. The story goes that this was one of the regular haunts of King James V when he was resident at Falkland Palace; he was fond of wandering about the countryside incognito as 'the guid man of Ballengeich' – a gulley at the foot of Stirling Castle used by the king as a secret exit. Many tales are told of the king's encounters with his subjects who failed to penetrate his disguise as he walked along the shores of the now drained Rossie Loch from which Rossie House takes its name.

The modern village of Collessie has several interesting 18th

An unexpected view down Kiln Heuch, Auchtermuchty, from the war memorial in the High Street. The house on the left is dated 1732 and the Boars Head Inn celebrates the time when the Stewarts and the Earls of Fife hunted boar in the woods around the old burgh once called *Uachdarmuc,* 'the high ground of the wild boar' *(D.C. Thomson & Co Ltd).*

and 19th-century weavers' cottages, a school and a manse, all clustering in narrow roads round the square towered church of 1839. In medieval times its neighbourhood supplied part of the living of the Abbey of Lindores and the See of St Andrews. Three houses are worthy of note in the area. Kinloch House, on the site of an earlier house of 1699, was owned by the Hutchison family and it was given to the Church of Scotland in trust to be used as an Eventide Home for the Elderly in 1956; Pitlour House is of 1674 with 1907 enlargements; and Rossie House is 18th century although the estate goes back to David I.

In medieval times wild boars rooted in the oaks, swamps and forests of Auchtermuchty and gave their name to the Pictish settlement called *uachdarmuc,* 'high ground of the wild boar'. Granted a charter in 1517, which elevated it into a Royal Burgh, Auchtermuchty today is a village of crow-stepped gables, red pantiles, thatched roofs and bridges, some dating from medieval times. Macduff House, named after a previous edifice on the site belonging to the Earls of Fife, stands on the west side of the main square and is the oldest house extant in Auchtermuchty dating from 1592. From this house, it is said, Lord Sempill was married to Mary Livingstone, one of Mary Queen of Scots 'Maries'.

Auchtermuchty's church was built in 1780 and enlarged in 1838, while the Tolbooth dates from 1728. The bell of the Tolbooth was said to be one of those purloined from Lindores Abbey at the Reformation. Formerly Auchtermuchty was known for its linen factories, bleachfields, distillery and sawmills, and today there is still light engineering and a deer farm at Reedie Hill said to be the first commercial red deer farm in Great Britain. Auchtermuchty is on record as having gone bankrupt in 1818 when creditors sold up the assets of the burgh. Today Auchtermuchty's most famous resident is the accordian player Jimmy Shand.

Sixteenth-century Myers Castle, enlarged in 1822 and 1890, was built by John Scrymgeour on the estate given by James I to his English page Robert Croxwell for faithful service. The castle was restored in the 1960s. Part of the old Myers estate now forms the village of Dunshelt, which some etymologists have described as a corruption of 'Dane's Hold', a local encampment of the Danes who were defeated at Falkland Moor.

CHAPTER 4

St Andrews and the Eastern Heartland

I. Fife's archiepiscopal city and university town – St Andrews

Most people enter St Andrews by way of the A91 from Guardbridge. First encountered, on the right, and rising towards Strathkinness, is the old estate of Kincaple which was under the governance of the Archbishop of St Andrews until 1587 whence it passed to the Crown and was partially gifted to James Melville, Constable of the castle of St Andrews, for his diplomatic services at the Danish Court. When the village of Kincaple was developed, its inhabitants were employed in the malt barns and brickworks and in the papermills of Guardbridge. Kincaple House was built by Alexander Meldrum in 1788 as Bloomfield Farm, and wings were added in 1927. At the other side of Kincaple village is the altered 17th-century house of Wester Kincaple. The old mansion of Kincaple was flatted in recent times with holiday chalets in its grounds, in which trees were planted in Napoleonic times. Plans are afoot to turn it into a golf club complex.

Before the A91 sweeps past the university's North Haugh complex, it passes Strathtyrum, another estate in ecclesiastical hands until the Reformation, and which too fell to the Crown and was conferred on the royal favourite, the Duke of Lennox. Archbishop James Sharp purchased the property in 1669, and thereafter it passed to the Cheape family who have owned it to the present day. The mansion house is much altered too, and it was rented in Victorian times from the Cheapes by John Blackwood (1818-79), the publisher, who regularly entertained such eminent figures as the historian James Froude, the writers Charles Kingsley and Anthony Trollope, and the painter Sir John Millais.

St Andrews' western approaches are dominated by its four golf courses and by the Old Course Hotel, opened in 1968. The earliest note on golf in St Andrews is dated 1552 and the oldest golf course in the world is the Old Course which was purchased by the Town Council in 1894. The New Course was constructed in 1895 by the Royal and Ancient Golf Club, and in 1912 the Eden Course was laid out by the Town Council who had already created the Jubilee Course in 1897 to celebrate Queen Victoria's Diamond Jubilee.

The game of golf as we know it today has its origins in Scotland, and St Andrews is the 'Mecca of Golf' bar none. Throughout the world the rules of the game are administered by the Royal and Ancient Golf Club, which had its origins in a meeting of some 22 Fife 'noblemen and gentlemen' on 14 May 1754. They formed themselves into 'The Society of St Andrews Golfers' to play annually for a silver club over the links at St Andrews, the winner to be 'Captain of the Golf'. During January 1834, King William IV agreed to be patron of the Club which thereafter was styled 'The Royal and Ancient Golf Club of St Andrews'. In those days the 'Union Parlour' then on the site of the old Grand Hotel (now the students' residence of Hamilton Hall) was used as a clubhouse. The present clubhouse was opened in 1854 and is commonly called the 'R & A', and remains a private club and is the Governing Authority for the Game of Golf through the greater part of the world.

The layout of St Andrews streets retains the features of a medieval town, and despite the extensive housing developments to the south, the burgh has changed little over the past 300 years. St Andrews is a perfect blend of wynds, courtyards, streets and closes conveying the mood of a typical old Scottish burgh. Golf, which brought wealth and status to St Andrews in the 19th century, is just a third of St Andrews' story, because long before the game began the town was conceived as a result of a saint's misfortune, if the medieval chroniclers are to be believed.

Over the sea they came to the land of the Picts. It was only a little ship, and they had travelled far. The Greek monk in the prow looked anxiously at the dark cliffs with their collar of turbulent surf. Yet, there where the sharp rocks gave way to a sand-duned bay, the dark clouds opened; the sun shone again and he knew he had found the place in the 'region towards the west, situated in the utmost part of the world' that his vision had foretold. Thus the medieval legend recounted how the

Winner Jack Nicklaus receives the trophy after his victory at the British Open Golf Championship, St Andrews, 1978. The Open Championship was inaugurated in 1860 at Prestwick, Ayrshire, and the first Open to be played at St Andrews was in 1873. The earliest note of golf in St Andrews is dated 1552, but the game was played elsewhere in Scotland as early as 1413 *(D.C. Thomson & Co Ltd).*

Greek monk, St Regulus, had journeyed from Patras with his holy treasure. For in the year 345 he had been warned in a vision that the Emperor Flavius Valerius Julius Constantius intended to remove the holy relics of the Apostle and Martyr, Andrew, and take them to Constantinople, then the capital of the Eastern Roman Empire. And so he collected an armbone, three fingers of the right hand, a tooth and a kneecap, and journeyed with devoted companions to the land of the *Picti* – those dark, painted folk who were to confer on Fife the status of a 'kingdom'.

The coming of Andrew's bones was to give Fife its unique position in the history of Scotland. Their enshrinement at St Andrews, 'the mother of all the churches in the Kingdom of the Picts', at the behest of Angus mac Fergus, High King of the Picts, ensured that the county was the political and ecclesiastical centre of Scotland until the 16th century.

The burgh of St Andrews was founded some time between 1144 and 1153 by Bishop Robert with the leave of David I. When the bishop established his burgh there had been a settlement, called *Kinrimund,* 'the head of the King's mount', with a religious community since at least the 8th century to link with that myth which tells us of the coming of St Regulus. St Andrews has long been referred to as 'The Canterbury of Scotland', and its ecclesiastical history can be traced in reality rather than myth to three phases of development. First there was the Celtic church which evolved through the missions of St Columba of Iona. For several centuries the Culdees formed a flourishing church, and at St Andrews they had a chapel on Kirkhill, rediscovered in 1860, above the harbour, with the foundations of a 12th-century nave and a 13th-century choir. In time the Culdee Church was superseded by the stronger Roman Catholic church, largely through the influence of St Margaret, Queen of Malcolm Canmore. This links with the cult of St Andrew, whose relics were first preserved in St Regulus' tower, the 10th-century stone-built tower which dominates the ruins of St Andrews Cathedral at the east end of the town. These relics remained in the tower for some 160 years until a more fitting repository was found for them behind the high altar of the new cathedral established a stone's throw away.

The cathedral of St Andrews was founded in 1160, consecrated in the presence of Robert I, the Bruce, in 1318 and despite the vicissitudes of fire and weather remained intact until that evil Sunday of 5 June 1559 when it was sacked by Presbyterian fanatics incited by a sermon of John Knox. The mob stripped the cathedral of its treasures, vandalised its sacred places and left it to decay; the central tower collapsed around 1586 and from 1559 to 1826 or so its stones were quarried for re-use elsewhere in the town. At its zenith the See of St Andrews had many fine church buildings. Abutting the cathedral was the Priory in which lived the Augustinian Canons who administered the cathedral and ministered to the people of Fife and beyond. Surrounding all is the precinct wall of

Once a formidable fortress and prison, St Andrews Castle was also a palace of the bishops and archbishops of the diocese. The first castle was erected here c.1200 by Bishop Roger, probably on the site of an earlier fortification. Most of the stonework seen today dates from the 16th century and the picture shows the 14th-century Fore Tower (left), the Sea Tower (centre) and the Kitchen Tower (right) *(Peter Adamson)*.

Prior Hepburn, and today the wall remains at over half a mile in length with thirteen towers and three gateways in addition to the 14th-century Pends, the main gateway into the domestic range of the cathedral.

The square tower in Prior Hepburn's Walls overlooking the sea is dubbed the 'Haunted Tower' and was found to have been crammed with human bones and coffins when it was opened in the 19th century. In the vicinity of this tower there appears, from time to time it is said, the ghostly figure of 'the White Lady . . . in a soft trailing dress and long, black wavy hair'. Should you put your hand through the arrow slit in the tower you are likely to shake hands with a ghost! Such stories, and many others like 'The Smothered Piper of the West Cliff' and 'The Veiled Nun of St Leonards', were collected by a former St Andrews Dean of Guild, William T. Linskill (1856-1929), whose vivid imagination and ghoulish 'howkings' in the cathedral precincts kept St Andrews spines tingling for many a year.

St Andrews had many other church buildings, though some have completely disappeared and others are in ruins. The aisle of the 16th-century Blackfriars' chapel remains in South Street, in the grounds of Madras College (1832), and the well of what remains of the 15th-century Greyfriars monastery is now to be found in Greyfriars Garden, which runs parallel with the wall which linked to the Marketgait port, one of the main gates into the medieval burgh. Holy Trinity church in South Street, opposite the Town Hall (1861), was built in 1412 to replace the 12th-century parish church whose site had been next to the south-east gable of the cathedral; the parish church in South Street was remodelled in the 18th century and 1907-09. The original tower of the church remains and inside is to be found the Dutch-built (1681) monument to the murdered Archbishop James Sharp. For the ecclesiastical architecture buff there is also the 15th-century chapel of St Leonard's College, reached down the Pends, and set by St Leonards School for Girls (1877).

In medieval times St Andrews was a town within a town, and it was divided into four quarters – those of the merchants, the fishermen, the prelates and the university, all set on the main highways which fanned out from the west door of the cathedral. Market Street, with its Tolbooth (demolished 1862), its buttermarket, Mercat Cross (removed 1768) and Tron, was the domain of the merchants. North Street had at its eastern end the Fisher Cross denoting the area of the fisher folk, and further down was the nucleus of the university, while the Scores linked with the medieval castle. South Street was a great processional way to the cathedral and down this wide street merchants built their houses many of which had 'riggs' or long narrow gardens, some of which have remained since they were first laid out in the 15th century. The recently restored 'Merchant's House' (49 South Street) is a fine example of such a dwelling which has late 16th-century painted ceilings.

The colour and splendour of St Andrew's medieval craft guilds and merchants is remembered each year in the town at the Lammas Market. The oldest surviving medieval market in Scotland, it takes place in early August and showmen come

This photograph by the distinguished St Andrews photographer George Cowie, dated 1947, brings to life the bustle and colourful sideshows of St Andrews Lammas Market. The oldest surviving medieval market in Scotland, it is held annually in early August and showmen come from all over Britain to set up their stalls. At the turn of the century is was a hiring fair for the ploughmen seeking work, but today it is a bright, cacophanous holiday carnival *(University of St Andrews: George Cowie).*

from all over the UK to set up stalls and shows in Market Street and South Street. Once held on 'the day of St Peter's Chains (1 August), the colourful and joyful religious overtones were swept away at the Reformation. At the turn of the century Lammas Market was a hiring-fair for ploughmen seeking work, but today it is a bright, noisy holiday carnival. One relic which many visitors miss is the 'Blue Stane', formerly set in the centre of the road. Once the rendezvous of the Whiplickers (the Carters) Society, on the day they held their annual races, the whinstone boulder is now set within the gardens opposite Hope Park Church (1864) in St Mary's Place.

At the end of The Scores, medieval Swallowgait, which derives its name from the old Scots *scaur* (a ridged clifftop), there stands St Andrews' courtyarded castle. Built around 1200, probably on the site of an earlier fortification, it has a long history of demolition and rebuilding and makes good use of the cliffs for its north and east defences. Down the centuries the castle's role has been fourfold – a fortress; a prison; an episcopal palace; and an archiespiscopal palace. The stonework seen today dates in the main from the last rebuilding by Archbishop John Hamilton of 1547-71. The castle contains the famous Bottle Dungeon of around 1386 and the mine and countermine dating from the siege of 1546-7. The castle declined in importance after the Reformation and in 1654 the Town Council ordered that part of the stonework be used to repair the harbour. As with the cathedral, and the cathedral museum set within the Prior's House, the castle is open to the public at standard times.

Outside the castle's main entrance, and set in the roadway, are the stone-block initials 'G.W.' – these are in memory of the Protestant reformer George Wishart (1513-46), the intimate friend and teacher of John Knox. Wishart was arrested by the order of Cardinal David Beaton (1494-1546) and was burned to death outside the castle for heresy; it is said that the Cardinal watched Wishart's incineration from a window of the castle on 1 March 1546. Wishart was probably involved in the attempted assassination of Beaton in 1544, and his fellow conspirators eventually murdered Beaton at St Andrews castle less than three months after Wishart's death. Beaton is thought by many to have been buried in the Dominican monastery of Blackfriars in South Street. At the Reformation this tomb would be destroyed, so vilified was his name in local memory. John Knox (c.1512-72) joined the Reformers in 1547, and when St Andrews castle fell to a French expedition he was sent to the penal galleys in France. The Protestant 'martyrs' have a high profile in St Andrews memorials, for instance on the Scores – above the Bruce Embankment – stands the Martyrs Monument of 1842, erected to the memory of Patrick Hamilton and George Wishart, and Paul Craw who was burned near the Market Cross in 1433, and Henry Forrest and Walter Myln who were burned on the north side of the cathedral in

St Andrews Cathedral looking towards the great east window before which, and behind the high altar, stood the shrine of Scotland's patron saint, the Apostle and Martyr, Andrew. The cathedral was founded by Arnold, Abbot of Kelso, in 1160, with the active assistance and encouragement of King Malcolm IV. The great cathedral church was consecrated by Bishop William de Lamberton in 1318 before a great multitude led by Robert I, the Bruce. The cathedral was famous throughout Europe until it fell into disuse at the Reformation in 1559. Behind is the square St Regulus or St Rule's tower of the earlier 11th-century cathedral *(Peter Adamson)*.

1533 and 1558 respectively.

Along from the castle, past the cathedral walls and down Kirkhill, the harbour has a pier nearly 300 yards long, and where the medieval fleet used to anchor there is a smattering of fishing boats and a plethora of pleasure craft in the 18th-century inner harbour. Originally there would be a wooden pier here, built around 1100, and a stone pier was built around 1560. Rebuilt in the 17th century with stone from the castle, the harbour saw the bustle of exports of grain, coal, potatoes and iron up to the 1920s.

Apart from golf, St Andrews today is essentially a university town, with the university as the main landlord and employer in the old burgh. The University of St Andrews is the oldest in Scotland and originated in 1410. A high standard of education was offered at the school attached to the Augustinian Priory of the Cathedral and a charter of incorporation was given to the school by Henry Wardlaw, Bishop of St Andrews, during 1411-12. The activities of this school were officially recognised by the Avignon Pope Benedict XIII in 1413 and thus the school became recognised as equivalent to the other prominent educational establishments in Europe. At first the university was no more than a society of learned men concerned with the study of Arts, Divinity and Canon Law. Within a few years they acquired their first building, the pedagogy in South Street on the site of the old University Library, and by the end of the Middle Ages three endowed colleges had been founded: St Salvator's (1450); St Leonard's (1512) and St Mary's (1537). Throughout the 16th century almost all of the leading figures of church and state in Scotland were educated in St Andrews.

At the Reformation the University was stripped of its 'popish' influences and was the centre of a new national scheme of education grounded in the parish schools. St Mary's College became a seminary of Protestant theology. University life was regularly interrupted by the political troubles of the 16th and 17th centuries. It survived through the burgh's decline of the 18th century and achieved a slow recovery in the 19th century when the town underwent a commercial revival. the University expanded rapidly from 1886 to 1915. Following a separation of Queen's College, Dundee to form its own university in 1967, the University of St Andrews is again limited to the town of its birth. The university buildings are easily viewed and a visit to St Salvator's collegiate church and tower, which dominate North Street, is particularly recommended. The church was built 1450-60 by James Kennedy, Bishop of St Andrews, and the spire was added to the tower around 1550. Within the church is the tomb of the Bishop, who is remembered too in a colourful pageant which forms a highlight of the university year.

Thought to originate in 1849 as an end-of-term 'rag' by final-year students, the Kate Kennedy Pageant is a colourful costume display in which sixty to seventy students (members of the Kate Kennedy Club) process through the streets dressed as

The tower of St Salvator's College, founded in 1450 by Bishop James Kennedy, soars above the bishop's Collegiate Church, cloisters and Quad of the United College of St Salvator and St Leonard of the University of St Andrews, the University itself originating in 1410. Extensively renovated in 1861 and 1930, the church remains as a fine example of Scottish ecclesiastical architecture and contains the tomb of Bishop Kennedy *(Peter Adamson)*.

characters associated with the town and university, from Mary Queen of Scots to Field-Marshall Earl Haig (a former Rector). The pageant takes its name from the following circumstances. The old bell in the tower of the collegiate church of St Salvator has long been known as 'Katherine', supposedly named after the niece of Bishop Kennedy. At the 'rag' one student is thought to have dressed up as 'Kate' and capered at the centre of the noisy masquerade. The 'rag' was successful and was repeated until it became a tradition. As the professors attempted to suppress it, the tradition became a symbol of undergraduate freedom. It was almost totally banned from

1874 to 1926 when it was revived as a historical pageant.

The matriculated students of St Andrews University have always had a say in the government of the university through their ancient right to elect a Rector. The Rector holds the position for three years, is the Chairman of the University Court and is spokesperson for the students both within and without the University. The students have been represented down the decades by famous Rectors like Andrew Carnegie, Sir James Barrie, the explorer Fridjof Nansen and the more recent 'media men' Tim Brooke-Taylor, John Cleese and Frank Muir. In 1982 the students elected their first female Rector in journalist Katherine Whitehorn.

Each street, wynd and close of St Andrews offers a great diversity of architecture to cater for all tastes, be it the 16th-century 'Roundel' at the east end of South Street or the newer buildings at the North Haugh. St Andrews too has its own theatre, the Byre Theatre, which evolved from the St Andrews Play Club in 1933, and the town still has a functioning cinema.

Many Americans visiting St Andrews for the first time are surprised at the town's many US associations. For instance, the American Declaration of Independence (1776) was signed by three *alumni* of St Andrews University; John Bain of St Andrews cast the first dollar sign ever used in America in 1797; Andrew Carnegie, as mentioned, was a Rector of the University; and E.S. Harkness of Cleveland, Ohio, was one of the university's most generous benefactors through the Pilgrim Trust.

Some of St Andrew's University's famous graduates include the famous poet William Dunbar (c.1460-1530) and Sir David Lindsay of the Mount (1490-1555), James Graham, Marquis of Montrose (1612-90), and the inventor of logarithms, John Napier of Merchiston (1550-1617). The quad of St Mary's College in South Street, incidentally, contains the famous Holm Oak tree planted around 1750, the 'Queen Mary Thorn' of around 1565, and the hall where the Scottish Parliament used to meet abutting the Old Library.

St Andrews further offers a wide range of walks to reflect both town and gown, and the Lade Braes Walk brings the country into the heart of the burgh. Access to this walk is opposite the West Port (1589) gateway at the west end of South

The famous 18th green of the Old Course, St Andrews has been the scene of many nail-biting golf tournaments and is known to golf enthusiasts worldwide thanks to the televising of the Open and of international matches. Overlooking the Old Course – the oldest golf course in the world – is the Royal and Ancient Golf Club, founded in 1754. The present clubhouse was opened in 1854 and is commonly called 'the R & A', but the club do not own the links *(Peter Adamson)*.

Street, on the south side of Argyle Street through the car park. The walk leads along the edge of Cockshaugh Park, and through the trees to the south is the University Botanical Gardens which are open to the public and are reached from the Canongate. Following the walk is the Kinness Burn which meanders to St Andrews harbour from its source by Kemback and Blebo Craigs. Lade Braes Walk offers a variety of ornamental as well as native species of trees from the Rowan and Lime to the red-leaved Sycamore and Ash. The wildlife content of the area is rich too with red squirrels and mallard as only two examples. Towards the end of the walk at Lawmill Cottage is the mill dating back to 1757 with its surviving mill wheel. Rising above the modern housing developments to the south is the Iron Age cemetery of Hallowhill.

II. Strathkinness – Kemback – Dura Den – Pitscottie – Ceres – Craigrothie – Hill of Tarvit

Strathkinness may be reached by taking the B939 out of St Andrews, which while it is in the old burgh, appears as Argyle Street, Hepburn Gardens and Buchanan Gardens. The houses comprise the mostly Victorian and Edwardian western development of St Andrews, and on the right are the University Playing Fields, the University Observatory and David Russell Hall, a students' residence completed in 1971. The visitor has a choice of roads to Strathkinness – the High Road which leads to the north end of the village, or the Low Road (B939) arriving at the south end. The High Road leads to the crest of the hill where there are magnificent views north across the Eden and Tay to the distant Grampian mountains. At night, when the air is clear, the lights of all the towns of the Angus coast can be seen as far as Arbroath.

The village of Strathkinness appears on record for the first time in 1144 when Bishop Robert gave the lands to the Priory of St Andrews and a settlement was established by 1160 nearer to the B939 than the modern village. After the Reformation the lands fell to the Balfours of Burleigh and they were forfeited to the Crown because the Jacobite Balfours were involved in the 1715 rebellion. The policies were purchased by the Melville family in 1724 and so remained until 1900 when the properties were sold to James Younger of Alloa. The Youngers built Mount Melville mansion house (1903) and in 1947 the grounds of the house were sold to Fife County Council and the mansion was used first as a maternity hospital and thence as a geriatric hospital; the grounds with the Dutch Model village (1918) and Japanese, English and Italian gardenscapes were made into Craigtoun Country Park. The park is signposted from St Andrews and Guardbridge and is under the management of the North East Fife District Council and was designated as a Country Park in 1976. Set within the park too, is the new Countryside Centre on the site of the old tennis courts. The display areas promote wildlife studies both of the park and the Eden Estuary; an audio-visual display on countryside topics is also featured. North East Fife Ranger Service is now based at the Countryside centre.

The Old Course Golf and Country Club was originally built as a hotel by British Transport Hotels in 1968 on the site of St Andrews' old railway yard. The hotel was sold to the English businessman Frank Sheridan in 1982, who carried out a £5m development, and the new golf and country club was opened in mid-1983 by the Princess Royal. The complex was acquired by P & O Ferries and in 1988 was sold to a consortium of international businessmen including the Royal and Ancient Golf Club *(Peter Adamson).*

Set on the hill in the form of a T, Strathkinness lay between medieval roads leading to St Andrews and was an agricultural community with a considerable amount of weaving too in the 18th and 19th centuries. Quarrying also was an important local industry up to modern times. A Free Church was established in Strathkinness in 1843 and the much altered church of 1867 is now the village hall. The parish church dates from 1864 and has also been greatly altered; the manse of 1873 is now a private house. Most dwellings are of the late 18th and 19th centuries, and there is still a Hearse House in which was kept the hearse to transport coffins to St Andrews for burial. The village still retains in situ four water pumps which have a unique place in the history of Scottish rural development.

To the south of Strathkinness lies Magus Muir over which the old Bishop's Road ran (the present B939 was not constructed until 1810 when the marshland was drained), and here, on 3 May 1679, nine Presbyterian fanatics hacked to death James Sharp, Archbishop of St Andrews and Primate of All Scotland. A former minister of Crail, Sharp threw in his lot with the Episcopalians on the reinstatement of episcopacy in Scotland. His act was anathema to the adherents of the Covenants who saw Sharp as a Judas. Today a cairn marks the spot where the archbishop was murdered, and nearby are the graves of one of the assassins and the Covenanters who were captured at the battle of Bothwell Bridge in 1679 and executed in revenge for the murder and for rebellion. Beyond Magus Muir is Drumcarrow Craig with its prehistoric settlement.

Strathkinness High Road continues along the crest of the hill overlooking Guardbridge and Dairsie to Kemback. The parish has as its focus the Gothic church of 1814, perched above Dura Den, close to its neighbour the post-Reformation church of 1582, which was originally a rectory given to St Salvator's College by Bishop James Kennedy in 1458. The people of Kemback once earned a living from the flax industry whose mills were powered by the Ceres burn in the gorge. The relics of this industry lie in ruins or have been converted to modern housing. Here lived Myles Graham, who was involved in the assassination of James I at Perth in 1437. The Schevez family obtained the estate of Kemback and in 1478 supplied an archbishop of St Andrews in William Schevez. Beyond Kemback wood and the gorge lies Blebocraigs, once the centre of 30 red sandstone quarries. The estate belonged to the Earl of Douglas in David II's time and in the 14th century fell to the Traills, a prominent son of whom was Bishop Walter Traill of St Andrews. Blebo House dates from the 19th century. Several paths crisscross this area, the haunts of many species of woodland birds from Blue Tits to Dippers. The yellow sandstone of Dura Den is particularly rich in fish fossils, and pioneer work in their collation was carried out by the geologist the Rev Dr John Anderson of Newburgh (see page 00). Old folk hereabouts used to tell how a man and a woman once sought refuge in the cave high on the cliff opposite Kemback Bridge and the 19th-century Mill House. There they lived until

Over a medieval bridge at Ceres marched an army which fought at Bannockburn with Bruce, the old tale states, but the 17th-century bridge in the photograph is remembered as the one over which Archbishop James Sharp's carriage rattled on the night he was murdered at Magus Muir in 1679. One of the few Scottish villages built around a village green, Ceres includes many buildings of note, especially the 1765 St John's Masonic lodge by the Auld Brig; the house was renovated in 1964. The 17th-century Weigh House nearby contains the Fife Folk Museum *(Peter Adamson).*

one day the smell of oatcakes burning accidentally on their fire brought their pursuers and the couple were murdered. 'To this day', the old folk confided, 'you can smell burnt oatcakes on the air from time to time at Kemback'. Kemback House has 19th-century gatepiers, a sundial of 1784 and a doocot of 1710, while the mansion is 18th century.

The road through Dura Den leads to Pitscottie and here lived Scotland's first vernacular prose historian, Robert Lindsay (c.1532-80), who wrote his credulous and picturesque *Historie and Cronicles of Scotland* covering the period 1436 to 1575. With its 18th-century bridge and a main crossroads formed by the B940 from Cupar and the B939 from St Andrews, Pitscottie was an old posting station. The B939 leads directly into Ceres.

First mentioned in the 12th century, in the reign of William the Lion, Ceres was formerly a burgh of barony within the control of the Hopes of Craighall, whose scion Sir Thomas Hope was the King's Advocate exiled by Charles I for his Covenanting sympathies, but recalled to public life by virtue of his legal wisdom. Weaving, bleaching, brewing and agriculture have all earned Ceres its daily bread, and a good place to start any exploration of the village is at the 17th-century Weigh House. This forms the entrance to an independent museum owned and administered by the Central and North Fife Preservation Society. Called Fife Folk Museum, the Weigh House once served as a burgh tolbooth and a venue for the pre-18th century Barony Courts; at the entrance is still displayed the *jougs* for the restraining of miscreants during market days. Above the doorway a stone tablet, set with the scales of a medieval merchant, contains the pious hope, GOD BLESS THE JUST, remembering both the law and fair dealing in trade. The museum, with its displays reflecting, in the main, Fife's economic and social rural activities, was opened in 1968 and the premises have expanded into adjoining pantiled cottages as the displays have grown. Within the complex is a delightful garden gallery and stonewalled terraces overlooking the Ceres Burn.

A stroll around Ceres reveals that its layout is a rare enough one in Scotland, a community around a village green. Near the museum, in the High Street, is the figure known as 'The Provost'. He sits, 'merry as a Toby jug', within his alcove and is local sculptor John Howie of Sauchope's conception of a church provost, the Rev Thomas Buchanan, the last holder of the office. Set beneath the statue is a Howie panel said to commemorate the Battle of Bannockburn in 1314; long lost in the garden of nearby Kirklands – the old manse – the panel was placed here in 1939.

Ceres church dates from 1806 and within its vestibule is a fine 15th-century crusader effigy which reminds us of the pre-Reformation church of St Ninian on the same site. The church spire was added around 1870. The 17th-century vault of the Earls of Crawford stands in the kirkyard. Ceres – perhaps a corruption of the medieval Latin *syrs,* a marsh – was long famous for its fairs, held in March and October, of which the 'Plack and Penny' fair was distinctive and was thought to date

A Royal Burgh of Robert I for sure since 1327, the centre of Cupar is seen down the Crossgate, looking towards the Mercat Cross and Bonnygate. On the left stands the public library, and the steeple of the Corn Exchange (1862) is to the right. Long known as 'the County Town of Fife', Cupar's old parish church of 1415 and 1785 is the oldest surviving foundation in the burgh. The County Buildings date from 1816 and 1925 and a railway station was first built here in 1847 *(Peter Adamson).*

back to the 14th century when the men of Ceres marched out with Sir William Keith of Struthers Castle to support Robert I, the Bruce, at Bannockburn. They crossed the ancient village bridge near to where Sir William had taught them archery at the Bow Butts, and across a successor of this bridge trundled the carriage of Archbishop Sharp only minutes away from his assassination. By the 17th-century bridge is the old house with its garden vaults known as St John's Lodge, once the house of the local Freemasons; it was built around 1765 and restored in 1964. Ceres' conservation area also includes Baltilly House (c.1780) and cottages. The village once had its own hospital which became a holiday home for underprivileged children, and this was to become the Rehabilitation Centre for the blind known as 'Alwyn House'. Ceres Games, which are still held, are thought to have derived from the celebrations after the victory at Bannockburn.

A stroll around Craighall Den – situated half-a-mile south of Ceres on the Largo road – is well worth the effort. Signposted from the centre of Ceres, the Den is a feast of horse chestnut and maple, beech and ash and the prehistoric hazel, all providing a habitat for fungi, small mammals and a wide range of woodland birds. Most of the Den and the site of Craighall castle were gifted to the local authorities by Col Hope of Luffness. Now vanished, the mansion of Craighall was built in 1637 by Sir Thomas Hope, incorporating French renaissance styles with the Scottish baronial of an earlier edifice. A prominent feature of the Den walk is the large lime kiln built in 1814 from stone from the ruin of Craighall Castle; the kiln, which manufactured lime to be used as fertiliser, went out of production in 1837. Beyond Craighall are the curiously named policies of Teasses (1879), and by Craighall Burn are the house (1750) and bridge (1769) of Teasses Mill.

The B939 leads out of Ceres to meet the A916 Cupar-Kirkcaldy road at Craigrothie, a village which was once a coaching stop. Craigrothie's old inn is 18th century and the earliest cottages hereabouts date from 1735; its mansion house is 18th-19th century, but the coach-house is dated 1668 and the Icehouse is contemporary with the mansion. Craigrothie's neighbour is Chance Inn, once known as 'Change Inn' because it was a stagepost where coach horses were changed for the last leg to Cupar. Some two miles to the south sits ruined L-plan Struthers Castle which dates from the end of the 14th century with 17th-century additions. Originally belonging to the Ochter-Struthers in the 12th century, the property fell to the Keiths, Grand Marischals of Scotland, and tradition has it, as we saw, that Sir William Keith led the archers and footsoldiers from Ceres onto the field of Bannockburn. In time the property belonged to the Lindsays and Crawfords and in 1633 the title of Lord Struthers was conferred on the first Earl of Lindsay. Charles I was entertained at Struthers in 1651, and two years later the castle was occupied by Cromwell's troops.

Between Craigrothie and Cupar are sited Scotstarvit Tower and the Hill of Tarvit. Scotstarvit Tower was also associated with the Struthers and is a five-storey L-shaped construction

The Douglas Bader Garden for the Disabled, Cupar – opened in 1982 by Group Captain Douglas Bader CBE, DSO, DFC, DL – is set by Duffus Park, itself the gift of the jute manufacturer J.C. Duffus, who donated the old Bonvil Park site to the burgh in 1911. Behind Duffus Park is seen Elmwood Agricultural and Technical College *(Peter Adamson).*

now cared for as an Ancient Monument and is open to the public at standard times. In 1627 Sir John Scott bought Scotstarvit estate and built his tower on the site of a previous building mentioned in a charter of 1579. A keen antiquary, the outspoken Sir John was Director of Chancery and author of *The Staggering State of Scots Statesmen,* containing illuminating comments on contemporary politicians and administrators,and he encouraged the study of topography in Scotland through sponsoring the work of Timothy Pont, finished by Sir Robert Gordon of Straloch and his son, and published in Amsterdam in 1654 by John Blaeu as an atlas of Scotland. He also edited *Delitiae Poetarum Scotorum,* an anthology of Latin verse by Scots (1637). Sir John's tower was abandoned in 1696 and his descendant, the Duchess of Portland, sold the estate to Oliver Gourlay of Craigrothie in the 18th century, and thereafter it was acquired by Col Wemyss of Wemysshill House, now known as Hill of Tarvit. When the Sharps bought Wemysshill in 1904 they commissioned Sir Robert Lorimer to enlarge the old house and lay out the surrounding gardens. The whole became a fine setting for the new owner's collection of French furniture. The house was bequeathed to the National Trust for Scotland by Miss E.C. Sharp in 1949 and the house and gardens are open to the public at set times.

The A916 links Hill of Tarvit with all the main trunk roads in Fife.

III. Cupar

No holiday in the Kingdom of Fife would be complete unless it includes a visit to Cupar, so noted the old guidebooks. And the traditional route of entry into Cupar by the West Port is still traced by way of the A91 from Stirling to the West. That medieval way carries the much-expanded modern traffic down Hangman's Road, past the ruin of Carslogie House (1590), erstwhile home of the Clephane family, into Cupar. On the left as the visitor enters the old burgh is Elmwood Agricultural College and Duffus Park. The Douglas Bader Garden for the Disabled stands in the park.

Elmwood Agricultural and Technical College today, incidentally, replaces two large houses, Elmwood and Hope Park, and temporary buildings, which were developed to supply the local need for further education colleges. From the 1920s evening classes in agriculture, horticulture, engineering and business studies were conducted at Bell Baxter Continuation School; these were switched to Elmwood House in 1953 and day classes were now offered. The new college was planned 1960-63 and commenced in 1968, to be officially opened in 1972.

In past days Cupar was the centre of the Judiciary for the County of Fife as well as being the county town; from the Middle Ages people came far distances to have their wrongs redressed at Cupar. Until the re-organisation of local government the old burgh was the administrative centre of Fife. From medieval times, too, Cupar was a prominent commercial centre; cattle and sheep were brought here for the flesher, hides for the cordwainer, wood for the tailor and weaver, and grain for the miller and baker. When financially

Cupar's Mercat Cross, seen in this photograph of c.1903, still stands at the junction of Crossgate and Bonnygate. The lamps were melted down for scrap in World War II. The shaft of the Mercat Cross, with its unicorn, was seriously damaged recently and removed. Dating from 1683, the cross was moved in 1788 to Wemyss Hill – to commemorate the treaty signed there in 1559 by the Queen Regent, Marie de Guise-Lorraine and the Lords of the Congregation – but it was restored to its original site in 1897 to commemorate the silver Jubilee of Queen Victoria *(G. Normand).*

embarrassed, kings sought help from the thriving little town run as a tight ship by the burgesses and enterprising Merchant Guild. In time the industries of Cupar concentrated around the making of linen, the milling of flour from the corn grown locally, and the processing of the cattle brought to market; only Cupar's cattle market remains. Once Cupar had a thriving trade with Holland, and from 1428 James II confirmed for the burgh the already established freedom of the Water of Eden and the right to use 'the Port of Mottray', modern Guardbridge, 'without any impediment or obstacle'.

Cupar was granted a charter as a Royal Burgh by Robert II in 1381, but the town has been a place of importance much earlier. Here in 1275 died Alexander III's wife Margaret, daughter of Henry III of England, and a year later Alexander held an assembly of the three estates: clergy, nobility and burgesses – forerunner of the Scottish Parliament.

For many centuries Castlehill, on which the Thanes of Fife has their stronghold, was the focal point of Cupar. Castlehill School of 1727 and 1846 is on the site of the ancient fortress, and here it is said that Sir David Lindsay of the Mount gave the first performance of his *The Satire of the Three Estates* (1535). J.G. Mackay, in his *History of Fife and Kinross,* leaves a picture of the first production: 'On the 7th of June at seven in the morning every man, woman and child who could get there gathered at Castle Hill and the play began. It consisted of seven parts or interludes loosely slung together. It took nine hours to perform, but the audience, who had breakfasted well in the old Scots style, were allowed intervals for refreshment and if they followed the advice of the messenger who announced the play, "With gude stark wyne your flagons see ye fill", they probably were well sustained throughout.' The performance was in the open air, so those who tired could leave, but probably few left so rare an entertainment, for Lindsay's satire went straight home to the thoughts germinating in the breasts of the people of those days. It cuts to the quick. It was a piece of history, and an acted sermon. As Scott said of Lindsay's work:

> The flash of that satiric rage,
> Which, bursting on the early stage,
> Branded the vices of the age,
> And broke the keys of Rome.

An English envoy who saw it performed before the Court at Linlithgow wrote that the King after seeing it 'called upon the Bishop of Glasgow, being Chancellor, and diverse other bishops and exhorted them to reform their fashions and manners of living, saying that unless they did so he would send some of the proudest of them unto his uncle in England'. A shock had been sent through society that day at Cupar.

Many of the landed gentry had their town houses in Cupar, like the Prestons of Preston Lodge (1623) and Lord Balmerino

Dairsie Bridge, across the River Eden, dates from c.1530, and on the brae above stand the ruins of the 16th-century castle (built on the site of an earlier fortress) and the church of St Mary built by Archbishop John Spottiswoode in 1621. Nearby, and up the hill, lies the village of Dairsie, full of cottages formerly the homes of linen weavers. Many of the weavers were Flemish, and they gave Dairsie its alternative name of Osnaburg, the coarse linen which had originally been brought from Osnabrück *(Peter Adamson)*.

in the Bonnygate (Boudingait of 1580) and the Earl of Rothes at Millgate in the Barony. Cupar's four old ports (town gates) have vanished, but the street layout to the north of the Eden is largely as it was in medieval times, Crossgate (medieval *Vicus Crucis* of 1505) and Bonnygate being the most ancient 'ways'.

Standing at the corner of St Catherine Street (the A91) is Cupar's Mercat Cross of 1683; it was placed here in renovated form to commemorate Queen Victoria's Diamond Jubilee in 1897. For decades the cross has stood at a site further into Crossgate, but at the end of the 18th century it had fallen into such a dangerous state of disrepair that it was to be broken up. The pillar and unicorn, however, were rescued by Col Wemyss of Wemysshill who caused it to be set up on Wemyss Hill to mark the spot where the treaty of 1559 was signed between the Queen-Regent Marie de Guise-Lorraine and the Protestant Lords of the Congregation; here it remained until 1897. Between the present site of the cross and St Catherine Street stood the old Tolbooth, and the story of its demolition is worthy of note as a tale of civic pride and unity between the burghers and the council. The Tolbooth had three floors; the lowest was a flat, foul, noisome den, almost entirely subterranean, which served as a jail and was known as the 'Black Hole'. The middle floor, called the 'Weigh House', contained the public weigh beam, while the top floor housed those imprisoned for debt. The debtors endured many hardships but were slightly better off than the miscreants at the lower level, but they depended for sustenance on the alms of charitable citizens which were placed in bags raised and lowered from the windows. The Provost of the day put forward the proposal that the whole dreadful place should be removed, but there was opposition from local law officers, and a messenger was sent to Edinburgh to secure an interdict from the Court of Session. In the meantime the Provost called up the burgesses who, by the light of torches and bonfires, destroyed the Tolbooth before the interdict could arrive.

A large part of the old town has been swept away at different times to satisfy the demands of 'modernisation', and these demolitions included the old closes and outside stairs that gave the town so much of its character. One relic of the past does exist, though, in the parish church. Records show that there was a church dedicated to the Blessed Virgin some distance to the north of the present site in Kirkgate. The church was in decay by 1415 and the church dedicated to St Christopher was erected on the present site; this was demolished in 1785 to make way for the present structure which was remodelled in 1882; the spire of 1620 remains. Nearby is the old churchyard which contains the severed heads of the Covenanters Laurence Hay and Andrew Pitulloch who suffered for their religious beliefs. Other buildings of note in Cupar are the County Buildings of 1816 and 1925, the Town Hall of 1817 and the steeple of St John's church (1877) and the Corn Exchange (1862).

Burgh schools were mentioned at Cupar from the early 14th

Said by some scholars to be the finest Romanesque church in Scotland, the church of St Athernase at Leuchars was built between 1183 and 1187 and was dedicated by Bishop de Bernham in 1244; a new nave was added to the church in the 19th century. On a knoll behind the church stood the castle of the Norman family of de Quinci who are said to have completed the church *(Peter Adamson).*

century and the modern Bell-Baxter School evolved from two local educational foundations, the Madras Academy founded by Dr Andrew Bell in 1831 and the education institute 'for young ladies' founded in 1871 by Lady Baxter of Kilmaron Castle. An interesting school, however, had been set up at the medieval Dominican monastery, which was located at the foot of Castlehill. Dedicated to St Catherine, the 4th-century Virgin and Martyr, the monastery was founded by Duncan, Earl of Fife, in 1348; the house was merged with the Dominican property at St Andrews in 1519 and the land of the friars was given to the burgh by James VI in 1572. It seems that nursery accommodation was located in the monastery precincts for the care and education of the royal children. The monastery buildings fell to Michael Balfour who was branded traitor in 1579 for his part in the murder of Henry Stuart, Lord Darnley, and thereafter the now-vanished monastery was the mansion house of the Lord of Balgarvie.

Cupar's railway station and bridge date from 1847, and by the bridge is one of Fife's very few public statues; this honours David Maitland Makgill Crighton of Rankeillour, born 1801, a well-known radical politician. Remembered too in the property known as 'The Chancellor's House' is John Campbell, son of the parish minister, who attained the highest legal office in Britain. Created Lord Campbell in 1841, he held the offices of Lord Chancellor of Ireland and Chief Justice of England, and became Lord Chancellor of Great Britain in 1859.

To the north-west of Cupar stands Kilmaron Castle, built in 1815 on the 15th-century estate of the Pitblado family by Admiral Maitland (see page 00) on ground long considered to be sanctified by the presence of a chapel dedicated to St Roan. The property was formerly the home of the educational philanthropist, Sir David Baxter of Dundee, who died at Kilmaron in 1872. Today the castle is in a state of advanced decay.

On the A91 out of the burgh, past the War Memorial (1922) and Braehead Park, lies Cupar's industrial estate set on the former site of the British Sugar Corporation's only factory in Scotland. The factory buildings, where sugar beet used to be turned into high-grade sugar, still survive. The A91 leads on to Dairsie and St Andrews.

IV. Dairsie – Balmullo – Leuchars – Tentsmuir – Guardbridge

Astride the A91 Cupar-St Andrews road, the modern village of Dairsie, with its 19th-century cottages, is set in rolling farmland and has a bustle about it. The village was formerly one of linen weavers, many from Flanders, and once Dairsie was called Osnaburg after the Flemish linen. It is thought that Dairsie was part of a 12th-century *thanage* with a church of that date rededicated to the Blessed Virgin Mary in 1243 by David de

A Spitfire of 602 Squadron sits at the main gate of Leuchars airbase, where it was formally dedicated in this ceremony in 1986. Aviation at Leuchars goes back to the time in 1911 when the Royal Engineers carried out experiments with balloons in the area. An airfield proper was developed during World War I when a Royal Navy Fleet Training School was established, and in 1920 Leuchars became an RAF station.

Bernham, Bishop of St Andrews. In historical terms the real focus of Dairsie today is to the south, down the byroads leading to Kemback. Standing above the River Eden, Dairsie Church and Castle are the historic core of the parish. The church, with its hexagonal belltower, remains essentially as it was when completed for John Spottiswoode, Archbishop of St Andrews, in 1621, although its roof was changed around 1800. Above the doorway is the armorial cartouche with the archbishop's coat of arms and the motto set in lead: *Dilexi de corum domus Tuae* – 'I have loved the habitation of thy house' from *Psalm 26.8*. The church was refurnished within in 1900. Today Dairsie folk worship in the plainer former United Free kirk (erected 1843, restored 1877) in the village, although from 1969 a group of individuals have kept an eye on the fabric of Spottiswoode's church. Dairsie mansion dates from 1828.

From the 13th century the bishops, and after 1475 the archbishops, of St Andrews had a residence at Dairsie; probably a fortified house on the foundations of the present castle abutting the church. Certainly a 'parliament' of nobles was held here in 1335, and it is said that David II spent part of his boyhood at Dairsie. In the 16th and 17th centuries Dairsie became associated with the Learmonths and Spottiswoodes who served the Crown and Church to great personal advantage. Archbishop John Spottiswoode rebuilt the late 14th-century bridge over the Eden, which had been restored by Archbishop James Beaton, and added towers to the castle to give it a Z-plan structure. It is said that the archbishop composed a large part of his *History of the Church of Scotland* (1655) at Dairsie Castle. Local folk have combined to consolidate the castle and policies to include a wooded walk to the river as a public amenity.

The A91 leads through Dairsie to a junction with the A92 and the latter leads to Balmullo past Pittormie on the left. The house dates from 1867 with a 1764 pediment, but the steadings are of 1855 and the Icehouse is dated 1862. On the hill above Muirhead stands the 16th-century L-shaped fortified house of Pitcullo restored for modern habitation in 1971. Balmullo sits at the foot of Lucklawhill and has become a popular dormitory village. The redstone quarry at the side of Lucklawhill is a landmark for miles, and paths and drives all over Fife are laid with Lucklaw chippings. At one time Balmullo was the home of Martin Anderson, who won national reputation as a cartoonist under the pseudonym of 'Cynicus'. He was one of the pioneers of the picture postcard and his factory at Tayport reproduced his satrical lampoons. The eccentric Anderson built his redstone Cynicus Castle as a folly on the grand scale and it had a commanding view of the area. Although the dwelling was never fully completed, Anderson packed it with treasures from Ancient Egypt. Anderson died in 1932 and his castle was demolished in 1939. Balmullo was formerly a popular place for holiday homes and was famous for its market gardens; some of the houses contained hand looms for the weaving of the locally grown flax.

Below Balmullo stands Leuchars Junction Station, across the

Earlshall Castle, a favourite hunting ground for Mary, Queen of Scots, was built in 1546 by Sir William Bruce. Today it remains a family home, open to the public at set times, displaying such treasures as the painted ceiling depicting the arms of Scotland's principal families and a plethora of mythical beasts. The gardens are set off by the famous topiary yews cut in the form of chessmen. The castle and gardens were restored by Sir Robert Lorimer in 1891 *(Maj. and Mrs D.R. Baxter)*.

Mottray Burn, which joins with the Moonzie Burn to empty into the River Eden at Guardbridge. Once the junction for trains to St Andrews and the East Neuk, Leuchars station won national fame when it was 'attacked' and set afire by suffragettes before World War 1. The village of Leuchars is now bypassed by the A919, but its historical jewel remains in the 12th-century church which is arguably the best Romanesque church in Scotland. Sited on a mound in the centre of the village, the church appears to have been built between 1183-87 and was dedicated in 1244 to St Athernase. The chancel and distinctive apse remain and a new nave was added in the 19th century; the church's arcaded decoration is a delight to see. Within is the memorial to Sir William Bruce who fought at the Battle of Flodden in 1513 and lived to found Earlshall castle in 1546.

Earlshall stands a half-a-mile to the east of Leuchars and is still a private home. In the 14th century this area was the estate of the Duke of Albany, as Earl of Fife, but in time part of it was granted to the Moneypennys of Pitmilly; the estate passed to the Hendersons of Fordell who sold the castle and estate in 1852. The whole fell into decay but was acquired by R.W.R. Mackenzie of Stormontfield who commissioned Sir Robert Lorimer to restore it. Earlshall is open to the public at set times and contains the distinctive long gallery with its painted ceilings showing the arms of the princpal families in Scotland and a myriad of mythical and fabulous beasts. Special exhibitions are set out in the Rod and Gun Room with its antique firearms and fishing tackle; the Museum Room displays family mementos, and the Royal Bedchamber with its period furnishings recalls the visit of Mary Queen of Scots in 1561. Outside, Earlshall gardens contain topiary yews in the form of chessmen and here, as within the castle, is an expanding collection of new exhibits. Earlshall is one of the most exciting restoration and refurbishment projects in Scotland. Incidentally, since the 400th anniversary of the execution of Mary Queen of Scots in 1587, Fife has been very much on the 'Mary Queen of Scots Heritage Trail': Earlshall, Falkland, Balmerino Abbey, Dunfermline Palace, Rossend Castle, can all be viewed from the perspective of Mary's life, as can St Andrews Cathedral, where her parents were nuptially blessed in 1538, and Queen Mary's House in South Street, St Andrews where she is thought to have stayed during her sojourns in Fife in 1561-65.

The old castle of the Norman de Quincys at Leuchars, which is remembered in the name of a farm, stood on a knowe to the north of the modern village, set within an area of once-treacherous marshes. The original wooden pallisaded motte and bailey was replaced with stone and rebuilt several times; the last castle here was torn down by the 6th Earl of Balcarres in the 1790s.

Today Leuchars is known for its RAF base and thousands of people come here annually for the air displays on the Battle of Britain Day. It was the Royal Engineers who started aeronautics here, when in 1911 they experimented with

Guard Bridge Paper Co Ltd, Guardbridge, taken from the air in 1958. The mill had its own railway sidings for coal deliveries; when the freight services were withdrawn at Guardbridge in 1966 a one-trip train serviced the private siding of the papermill for a little time until the whole branch was closed in 1969. Now a part of the US-based James River Corporation, under the name of GB Papers, the company is one of the acknowledged leaders in the printing and writings section of the UK paper market *(GB Papers)*.

balloons. During World War 1 an airfield took shape and the Royal Navy started a Fleet Training School here; in 1920 this was taken over by the RAF. By 1938 Leuchars airfield became fully operational as a base for Coastal Command, and it so remained until 1950 when it was transferred to Fighter Command; 1968 saw it evolve as Strike Command.

Across the Lundin Burn, and surrounded by the Tay, St Andrews Bay and the estuary of the River Eden, Tentsmuir was a wild, marshy and isolated region which the medieval chronicles filled with *diaboli, urses et bos primiginius* – 'devils, bear and oxen'. Tentsmuir was an area inhabited by Stone Age and Bronze Age man whose chief diet was mussels and clams; indeed the banks of the River Eden have a long history of mussel cultivation, used as bait by fishermen in many parts of East Scotland. In time Tentsmuir was inhabited by shipwrecked mariners and became a sanctuary for vagabonds and outlaws, including some from the Continent. The courtiers of Malcolm

Canmore hunted here out of their castle at Leuchars and introduced the rabbit which was in time to earn the estates of Scotscraig, Reres and Kinshaldy some £900 a year. The area was taken over by the Forestry Commission and is now one of the largest areas of woods in the county with visitor facilities at Kinshaldy. Tentsmuir has been chosen as the site of an astronomical observatory in which a gravitational wave detector will contribute to the future of astronomical research.

Guardbridge sits at the estuary of the River Eden, and takes its name from *gaire,* the triangular piece of ground hereabouts. The six-arch *gaire-brig* was built here, at great expense, by Henry Wardlaw, Bishop of St Andrews and, with its repairs of 1685, it remains a good example of a Scottish medieval bridge. On either side are panels bearing the arms of James Beaton, Archbishop of St Andrews. A modern bridge was built alongside in 1939 and the piers of the old railway bridge to St Andrews (line closed in 1969) are still to be seen. In this area was a gathering place for medieval pilgrims so that they could journey to St Andrews under guard through the wild places of Kincaple, now civilised by the A91.

The Guard Bridge Paper Co Ltd was founded in 1873 and was set on the site of the old Seggie distillery which had been founded by William Haig around 1810. From 1898 to 1960 the company reclaimed land from the River Eden and the Mottray Burn to make up the modern complex. Most of the workforce used to live in the village created here by the company between 1887 and the late 1930s. The new industrial 'laird of the manor' (the company managing director) lived at Seggie House above the village (the house is now a hotel). The mill was modernised in the 1960s and merged with Culter Mills Paper Co Ltd. Today the mill is owned by GB Papers, a subsidiary of the James River Corporation of Richmond, Virginia, USA.

CHAPTER 5

The East Neuk and its Neighbours

I. Boarhills – Kingsbarns – Crail

'I never saw so many good houses of people of family and fortune as in this part of Fife.' So wrote Sir Walter Scott of the East Neuk. He visited the area in June 1823, with Sir Henry Raeburn and the Blairadam Club. Today, the East Neuk has changed relatively little in aspect since Scott's time, but Sir Walter would hardly recognise the descendants of the folk he knew.

The A918 from St Andrews lies almost parallel to the coastal path to Crail, now developed as a nature walk. The trail runs by such volcanic rocky outcrops as the Maiden Rock, the Rock and Spindle and Buddo Rock and has exit points at Boarhills and Kingsbarns. This coastal walk is a fine place to study the flora and fauna of the area, from the red, green and brown seaweeds, the bivalve razor shells and cockles, to the profusion of kestrels, yellowhammers, herons and sedge warblers. Once this area was swampy forestland of oak, pine and beech; and from the time of the 8th-century Pictish monastery at St Andrews, wild boar, deer, wolves and bears were hunted by both prelate and laird alike on the Boar's 'Raik', or Run. Today, Victorian and Edwardian hands have transformed the few farm buildings along their route. The houses of Kingask and Pitmullen show a characteristic feature of habitation in East Fife – a big house and estate which once gave life and employment to a small village.

Round by Kinglassie, on a Sunday morning, the bellcote of the church at Boarhills bids the visitor welcome to the East Neuk, 'neuk' being the old Scots word for niche, nook, or corner. Boarhills church is set on the ridge of a hill just off the road before the sharp turn-off to the village proper. Once the folk of the area worshipped in the schoolhouse of the village, but in 1866 it was decided to build a church to serve the parish in 'keeping with the tastes and requirments of the age'. The church was set alongside a cemetery, which pre-dated it by many centuries; it was linked with the parish of Dunino in 1966. The older gravestones near the west wall of Boarhills cemetery emphasise the local sense of mortality. Drownings were a common occurrence along these shores. The most famous was the wreck of the Swedish brig *Napoleon* off Boarhills in 1864. All hands perished and lie with this Victorian sentiment above:

> The waters compassed me about even to the soul
> The depths closed me round about
> The weeds were wrapped about my head.

Just north of the church, at Chesterhill, was erected the first lifeboat station in these parts. Its early presence, it is uncharitably said, owed nothing to humanitarianism; the guidfolk of Boarhills 'negotiated' with the shipwrecked and would rescue only those able and prepared to pay! One chronicler actually accused the Boarhills folk up setting up false beacons to encourage wrecks!

Boarhills itself is a scattered parish. The land around rises and falls gently in this barley and potato-growing corner of Fife where the forests act as springboards for the foraging starlings, seagulls and greenfinches. Bypassed by the main road, the centre of Boarhills is tree-filled and tranquil. Dated 1789, Boarhills Primary School was taken out of the hands of the heritors in 1928 and was absorbed into the county system. The heritors of Fife's schools in past ages had a wide range of responsibilities from employing and paying the schoolmasters to succouring the poor. The school still has its bellcote, but the bell is displayed within the classroom.

The delightful country mansion of Kenly Green derives its name from the *ken* (promontory) made here by Kenly Water. Above the polluted stream, where salmon were once rifle-shot as they lept the weir which had been dynamited some time before by the Marines, two manmade hillocks invite the archaeologist's spade. Maybe one of them is the lost castle of Draffan, which the Rev James Roger averred was built here by the Danes. The 20-odd acres of wooded policies, with walled garden and tennis courts, haunt of roe-deer, lie partly in the old parish of Kingsbarns and partly in the parish of St Leonard and St Andrew, recalling they were monastic acres of medieval

Crail's Mercat Cross was re-sited in Marketgate in 1887 as a symbol of the burgh's corporate authority. Behind stands the burgh Tolbooth, its lower courses dating from the sixteenth century. Repaired in 1957, the Tolbooth still contains its fine Dutch bell of 1520 which originally hung in the church belfry. The Town Hall and the 1814 Council Chamber replaced a building of 1612.

times. In front of the house, across the burn, the Prior's gabled doocot is the oldest building hereabouts. Yet, by the time the present house was built in 1791, the land had come into the ownership of the university. It is believed that the house is on a much earlier foundation, a hunters' shelter, or a pilgrims' retreat. Designed by the Adam brothers, Kenly Green House exhibits their characteristic decorations and mantlepieces. From the 1920s, Kenly Green was the home of Sir Alexander Nairne Stewart Sandeman, jute spinner of Dundee and Liberal MP (1923) for the Middleton and Prestwich Division of Lancashire. When he died in 1940, the house fell to his widow and thence her relatives; since 1960 it has been modernised with care and taste. Near the front door is a hunk of Gothic masonry from the old Palace of Westminster, brought by the redoutable Sir Alexander.

All over the East Neuk ruined farm cottages, windows and doors agape, wantonly display intimacies of past life around the couthy hearthstones. Layers of peeling wallpaper tell of the labourers' fight against damp, and the nettle-ridden earth closets tell their own story. These privies were as good an indication of the character of the owners as anything. Some were noisome holes, others passably decent; while others had seats scrubbed to snow-whiteness and the wooden floors polished. A guidwife might even go so far as to nail up a popular Victorian religious text on the back of the privy door, like 'Thou God Seest Me'. Or impale a wholesome, inspiring scene like 'Bubbles' or 'The Light of the World'. The East Neuk inhabitant of past ages was nothing if not continually bent on broadening the mind.

On from Kenly Green the road to Crail swings past the Gallows Law, where miscreants, guilty or innocent, kicked their heels into eternity. Falside Farm lies on the right, and facing the road is an intriguing agricultural relic in the lee of the modern farm buildings: conical horse mills were once a common sight in Fife. Horse mills are low, circular or octagonal buildings with conical roofs, which used to house and protect the timber horse engine that drove the threshing drum in the adjoining barn. Generally the Fife horse mills had several openings, usually spanned by a timber ring-beam, in turn supporting a very intricate core of roof timbers. The rafters diminished in size towards the apex of the roof in the older examples, and are clad with slates on the outside and usually finished in a large simple knop finial. Internally the horse mill would be dominated by a large, square cross-beam traversing the centre of the mill parallel to the barn wall. This beam was formerly used to support the central shaft of the engine. On the floor would be a corresponding soleplate to take the base of the shaft. At one time horse mills were an essential part of a farm's economy, replacing the tedious job of threshing by flail and allowing larger quantities of grain to be threshed and cleaned by a smaller labour force.

Next to Falside is Pitmillie, now only represented by its lodges. These policies were owned in the 12th century by the priors of St Andrews Cathedral, and in the 13th century by the Monypennys, who were lairds for over 700 years. There is a persistent local legend that the family received its name from Malcolm Canmore. In the days when Malcolm was fleeing from the wrath of Macbeth, the king asked a stranger for the loan of a few pennies. The stranger replied, 'Nae sire, no a few pennies, but mony pennies.' When Malcolm triumphed he officially dubbed the stranger Moneypenny and endowed him with properties. The direct line of the Monypennys died out in 1974 and the mansion was converted into a hotel. Pitmillie was demolished when the latter enterprise failed. The estate is remembered in its weather jingle:

> Blaw the wind where it likes
> There's bield about Pitmillie dykes.

Kingsbarns is divided into two of the old land 'quarters', North and South. Originally called North Barns, the village became Kingsbarns after the extensive barns, now vanished, which were used to store the monarch's grain for use at Crail or Falkland Palace. Land here was given to the Black Friars of St Andrews in 1519 and dues from it supported Dominican friars who preached at St Monans and Dominican students at the university. In 1592 James VI bestowed the land on his former family nurse Helen Little in gratitude. The original church of Kingsbarn was built in 1631 when it became dissociated from that of Crail: the church was enlarged in 1811. The old manse (1847), now called West Lodge, has been divided into two private houses and lies behind the Primary School (1822). The church spire, which was added in 1865-66, has circular windows, some blind, and show the marks of many hands.

Next to the church is the Cambo Arms Hotel, really an inn, the earliest parts of which are contemporary with the church. The hotel has an unusual double front door. Once there were some twelve hostelries in Kingsbarns. Opposite the hotel, at the head of Station Road, is the whitewashed partially crow-stepped dwelling known as the Pleasaunce; dating from 1703, it is the oldest inhabited house in the village. Most of the modern village lies between the A918 and the sea, reached by Seagate and Sea Road at the south end of the village. The square is still extant with its pump of 1831, and leads to well-kept examples of East Neuk cottages, some given awards for restoration. The village owes much to an 18th-century laird called John Corstorphine who built Kingsbarns House in the square for his own use in 1794. Kingsbarns was Fife's first

Conservation Area.

Once, the partan (crab) yawls put into Kingsbarns but the village was formerly known for its Osnaburg sheeting and shirting. Down by the seashore can be seen the relics of the breakwater made by a local farmer in the late 19th century for the purpose of shipping potatoes to England. Probably the breakwater and the dykes of the fields were built from the stones of the now vanished Castle of Kingsbarns, which lay to the west of the coastal walk to Crail as it skirts the flat rocks known as The Coupit.

Along the A918, in the hallway of the Erskine family home at Cambo House, the Fife Hunt gazes collectively from the montage of the 1880s, and in a corner of the picture is a lively cameo of what Cambo House used to look like before the disasterous fire of 8 July 1878. The old house with its central tower was swept away, and Wardrop & Reid's design of 1879 remains, although it was divided into flats in the late 1950s. Functioning as a country estate, Cambo is angular and Victorian with little real character except its horological tower, the last resting-place of Kingsbarns' old clock. Cambo, once linked with Kellie, was a 12th-century foundation and stronghold of the Norman de Cambhous. The Myretouns held it from 1364 to 1668 when Sir Charles Erskine, Lord Lyon King of Arms, bought the property; the Erskines have lived here ever since.

The steadings of Cambo pre-date the mansion house, and folk still remember their ancestors who looted the Erskine wine cellars in 1878 while the laird's house burned merrily. The East Neuk fishermen were drunk for weeks on the best of the French vineyards. Set at a distance from the house is a Regency mausoleum, containing the tombs of the Erskine family and the Earls of Kellie. The estate's East New Hall Steading has been converted as the nucleus of a nature trail and visitor centre.

Associated with the history of Cambo are the boundary-linked estates of Randerston and Wormiston. There was an estate and castle at Randerston in the 13th-century owned by Sir John de Randolfstoun. The present house was built in the 16th century, a farmhouse variant of the L-plan. Along the main road to Crail, now almost hedgeless, are the policies of Wormiston. Today the house which bears the name has a 14th-

John Knox and Archbishop James Sharp both preached in Crail's Auld Kirk which stands at the east end of Marketgate. Dating from the mid-12th century, the Church of St Mary was expanded in the 16th century to include a belfry and a spire for the tower. Renovated in 1963, the church has many impressive 17th-century monuments in the kirkyard, with its fine memorial gates remembering the dead of both World Wars.

century foundation with its main architecture being of the 16th century with 19th-century additions. The property belonged to the Spens family who were Constables of Crail. Once the Spens lived in Crail Castle, but when this was abandoned the family took up residence at Wormiston, the centre of the crown barony. The house was owned sporadically by the Balfours and the Earls of Lindsay who sold the property in the 1950s to Lady Erskine as a dower house; she died here in 1958 and for nine years the house was empty until it was bought by an Edinburgh architect who renovated the property.

The best place to start an exploration of contemporary Crail is at the Museum at 62 Marketgate; it was opened in 1979 and is set in an old house which was first renovated in 1876. Above the door of the house, which stands sparklingly re-done in the shadow of the old Tolbooth, is the marriage lintel marked TM and IP and dated 1703. The town's information centre is next door.

Artists first discovered Crail in Victorian times, but the town was a royal burgh from 1310 to 1975. Its charter was confirmed by King Robert I, and it gave the burgh the right to trade on the Sabbath, a custom which the Reformers had a tough struggle to stamp out. Crail, of course, was old in the 14th century, for the nucleus of a burgh around the harbour was already in the ownership of Countess Ada de Warenne, mother of Malcolm IV and William I, in the 1160s. From holiday resort and medieval port trading with the Low Countries, to an ecclesiastical suburb of St Andrews, Crail has been a portal to European riches and ideas. Crail, meaning 'corner town', was once known for the longevity of its inhabitants. By the 16th century Crail had filled with handsome stone-built houses belonging to the merchants and neighbouring lairds secular and ecclesiastical.

For centuries Crail had an air of isolation about it. St Andrews was two hours away by coach, so the Crail folk had more knowledge of the countries represented by the sailors who came to haven here than they had of their fellow countrymen. The railway came to Crail in 1886 (the old station is now a garden centre) and brought a sense of wider horizons which had not been known since the town lost its monopoly as the fish market for Forth and Tay catches.

The A918 leads into the heart of the town, its eastern entry forming the High Street and Westgate. Facing the visitor is the white bulk of the early 18th-century Golf Hotel. Marketgate leads off from the A917 to run parallel with Nethergate. In Marketgate the much-altered 17th-century Dutch-influenced Tolbooth was set in the old market, which was one of the largest in medieval Europe. On the thick-set tower of the Tolbooth, with its pagoda-like roof dating from the 18th century, sits a fish weathervane as a constant reminder of the famous Crail Capon (a haddock, split and dried) which made the burgh celebrated. The Tolbooth bell was made in Holland in 1520 and once belonged to the church. The bell still rings the curfew at 10 o'clock.

In Marketgate, across from the Mercat Cross with its unicorn and 17th-century shaft (sited here in 1887), are the Regency town house of the Inglis family called Kirkmay (1817) and the much earlier and well-preserved Friar's Court (1686), restored in 1938. Marketgate is also graced with a memorial fountain celebrating the Diamond Jubilee of Queen Victoria. The medieval church and its officers are well represented in Crail's place names: Prior's Croft, Prior's Doocot and Prior's Well, hint at the priory of St Rufus and the properties of the nuns of Haddington in Nethergate. Now a treelined and peaceful backwater, Nethergate used to be lined with weavers' cottages, and around the greens of the town were once spread the bleaching yarns and cloths.

Crail's parish church, the old Kirk of St Mary, was first consecreated in the 13th century, but has been considerably altered particularly in 1796, 1815 and 1963. It became a collegiate church in 1517, had nine altars and was rich in ornamentation, vestments and books. In June 1559, John Knox preached in the church and the kiss of death was placed upon its ecclesiastical heritage. Within the church lobby is the Sculptured Cross dating from the 9th century. Near the kirk gate stands the Blue Boulder, a rock, legend has it, flung by the Devil from the Isle of May to demolish the church which was being built. The Earl of Hell missed and the boulder split in two, one part landing at Balcomie beach and the other where it is now – it still exhibits his dark lordship's thumbprint! At the kirk gate too once stood a school, demolished in 1890. Sir William Myretoun founded two schools in Crail in the 1500s where music and grammar were a particular forte. Crail once had five schools.

Crail's most ancient neighbourhood is around the harbour. Above the harbour the royal castle of David I stood threateningly until the walls fell into the sea. Here the king feasted on '9850 herrings and two porpoises' on one occasion, and made a special pilgrimage on 18 December, the feast day of St Rufus of Antioch, whose name blessed the castle chapel. The site of David's castle is now a flatted Victorian mansion. The King's Mill was sited next to the harbour.

The origins of Crail harbour are lost in antiquity, but there have been extensive repairs to it since the 1500s, and the west pier was added in 1826-28 to the design of Robert Stevenson. Up to the 1930s German sailing boats visited Crail with cargoes of timber and took home holds of potatoes.

Fronting the principal quay is the crow-stepped Custom House of the 1690s, which was repaired by the Crail Preservation Society in 1964. This relic of the excisemen who chased the fleetfooted smugglers through Crail's harbour vennels was acquired by the National Trust for Scotland. Crabs and lobsters are still offloaded at Crail. All around are the relics of centuries of Crail craftsmen. Spinning lint-yarn was an 18th-century cottage industry in Crail, but coal was once mined here and shoes were made. Crail craft market was legendary: pots, cloths, silverware, copperware, wood and leather objects were all sold and displayed in booths presided over by the various deacons of the crafts and guilds. These days craftsmen are few, but a pottery was set up in a 17th-century range of buildings in Nethergate in 1965. Here are workshops, kilns, clay plants all set off by a quaint yard under fruit trees.

In Victoria Gardens, St Andrews Road (A918), is the early Christian relic known as the Standing Stone of Sauchope dating from the 9th century. It was removed to this location in 1929. The gardens were opened on 1 July 1914 and were presented to the town by an expatriate, one George A. Gay of Hartford, Connecticut. Sauchope, now a caravan park, was Crail's first 'modern' golf course, laid out as nine holes in 1928. Golf had been played at Crail long before that, for the Crail Golfing Society is the seventh oldest club in the world and boasts that it is one of the very few clubs to have a compete set of minutes from its inception. The institution of the Golfing Society was set out simply: 'Several gentlemen in and about the town of Crail, who were fond of the diversion of Golf, agreed to form themselves into a Society to be known by the name of Crail Golfing Society. The Society was accordingly instituted upon the 23rd day of February 1786'. The prime competition of the Club is the Ranken Todd Challenge Bowl, and the area from which teams may be invited to play is restricted between Pitmilly Burn and the River Leven, reflecting the extent of the jurisdiction of the burgh as laid down by the Royal Charter of Robert I in 1310. The tournament format is thought to be unique to Crail.

From Marketgate the main road leads to Fife Ness, the most easterly part of Fife. On the approach, the old airfield lies to

The oldest part of the ancient burgh of Crail is the area around its castle site and the harbour. The main quay was old when repairs first started in the 16th century; the west pier was added in 1826-28 to the designs of Robert Stevenson. The white crowstepped Custom House dates from the 17th century and stands foursquare at the quayside, still a favourite haunt of artists, photographers and television drama producers.

left and right. This was a busy airport during World War I, and was a Royal Naval air station in World War II, with the name *HMS Jackdaw.* In 1946 it became Scotland's Royal Navy Boys' Training Estate, as *HMS Bruce,* and was closed in the 1950s. The provosts of Crail once added 'Rear-Admiral of the Forth' to their civic titles.

As the road bends right, Balcomie Castle, centrepiece of a modern farmstead, lies to the left. Privately owned and not open to the public, Balcomie Castle is an E-plan structure of the late 16th century with a 19th-century mansion and agricultural complex attached. The fine gatehouse remains, decorated with interesting panels showing the arms of the Learmonth family, and the Myretouns.

Fife Ness, a now vanished settlement, is best explored on foot, with parking at Balcomie Golf Links. Balcomie Golf Course is set in classic links with a little parkland and was first used by the Crail Golfing Society in 1895, its clubhouse on a commanding position offering panoramic views of the North Sea. At Craighead farm the road sweeps round to the Coastguard Station; where the road skirts the farmstead, the Dane's Dyke runs down to the sea. Popularly ascribed to Danish invaders, the dyke once enclosed the whole promontory of Fife Ness. At the sea end of the dyke Long Man's grave marks the supposed tomb of a Danish hero.

Round Foreland Head, towards Lochaber Rocks, the old anchorage can be seen where Marie de Guise-Lorraine, the bride of James V, landed on 10 June 1538. She rested for a few days at Balcomie Castle on her way to St Andrews for her nuptual blessing in St Andrews Cathedral. This was in the days when Fife Ness was a royal burgh through the new owner of Balcomie, Sir James Learmonth of Dairsie, who was a joint master of the Royal Household with Patrick Wemyss of Pittencrieff. Out to sea the North Carr Beacon gives light and sound warnings to shipping. These rocks have claimed many vessels and lives, the most famous wreck being that of the passenger steamer *Windsor Castle* in 1844. All around are relics of the salmon fishing cottages, and here is a good spot to observe the birds of Fife Ness which include the all-the-year-round inhabitants, the cormorants, the shags, the eider ducks and the dunlins, and the mainly August to May visitors, the turnstones. One should look out too for Constantine's Cave, with its walls decorated with incised crosses and primitive animals. Constantine II, King of Alba (903-943), became an Abbot of the Culdee monastery at St Andrews.

About three miles from Crail is Airdrie House, whose 14th-century policies became a major seat of the Lumisdaines. The privately owned Airdrie House of today incorporates the tower of the castle of 1586 and has seen much modernisation and was probably originally a hunting lodge for Crail castle.

II. Kilrenny – Cellardyke – the Isle of May – Anstruther – Pittenweem – St Monans – Elie – Earlsferry

The A917 hugs the coast from Crail to Anstruther and a few hundred yards along the way to Kilrenny it passes the old Salt Pans. All over Fife (and on the far left here at Sypsies) are ruined dovecotes – doocots to the Scots. In past days, incidentally, only the lairds of the manor could have a dovecote. Unmoved by the beauty of pigeons in flight, the laird erected his doocots for strictly practical purposes: ensuring a supply of fresh meat in the shape of squabs, or young pigeons, which could be easily lifted from the stone nesting compartments; wood pigeons were not easily taken otherwise before the coming of the shotgun.

Fishing and agriculture gave Kilrenny its character and the street names show the old structure of the village. Kirk Wynd led to the commercial heart of Trade Street which once rang with the hammers of the farriers and shoemakers. Yet most folk worked on the land and lived in the cottar houses like those in the curiously named Routine Row – undoubtedly a corruption of *Route de roi,* 'king's way'. Kilrenny once had political importance in that it had its own MP in the Scottish Parliament. In 1578 the village was given a charter by Partick Adamson, titular Archbishop of St Andrews, to erect a market cross and hold a weekly fair. Here in Kilrenny in 864 a chapel was dedicated to St Ethernan, a companion of St Adrian of May Island. Once, the landlords of the area were the monks of Dryburgh Abbey, who were given the policies of *Kilrethni* by Ada de Warenne around 1177. They sponsored a church on the site of the ancient edifice, and it was re-dedicated in 1243. This church was demolished in 1808 when the present one was built. It was renovated in 1933 and retains its plain interior, but with a fine reredos.

Abutting the foot of the tower is the huge 18th-century tomb of the Lumisdaines of Innergelly, and around the corner is the equally massive mausoleum set up by the Duchess of Portland in memory of her father, General Scot of Balcomie. Local legend has it that the despised bones of the murdered Cardinal David Beaton lies somewhere around, brought here by his nephew John Beaton of Balfour in 1546.

Modern Kilrenny is quiet and gains much from being bypassed. Across from the church the old school is now the church hall, and opposite in Main Street a newly renovated house has the marriage lintel for GB:EB 1644; yet the stonework predates the lintel which likely has come from afar. Kilrenny's old manse is not in the heart of the village, but lies across the main road: built in 1818, it stands foursquare and stolid with a part-moat effect. Some windows are blocked up, not as is popularly supposed to avoid window tax of 1697-1851, but simply according to an incumbent's wishes. A picnic area has been set out down Common Road, placed between two lectern-type doocots.

The 'big hoose' at Kilrenny is Innergelly which was part of the marriage dowry of Annabella, wife of Robert III, and it became the home of the Beatons. Subsequently owned by the Barclays of Kippo, the property was purchased by Sir James Lumisdaine of Airdrie estate. The present mansion, dating from 1740, with its statue of Hermes (Mercurius to the Romans) high above the pediment with a coat of arms of 1630, became the home of the Sandys-Lumisdaines from 1830 and the family occupied the house until the 1960s. The Skeith Stone near Rennyhill farm was set up to commemorate the defeat of Danish invaders by the men of Kilrenny. It depicts an eight-pointed cross and takes its name from the Scots words for injury.

Up to 1641, Cellardyke (and Anstruther Easter) were included in the parish of Kilrenny, to which village there is still a coastal link-road via Basket Road and Kilrenny Mill. Once called Nether Kilrenny, and Skinfasthaven, Cellardyke's modern name is easy to fathom. Cellars were built at the foot of the hill by Kilrenny folk to accommodate their fishing tackle, thus saving them a stiff lug up the braes. The dykes were added on the cliff to protect the drying fishing nets from the hungry cattle and goats.

Approaching Cellardyke's heart from the turning off the A917, the road passes Anstruther Holiday Village, built on the site of the RAF station of the 1940s and 1950s. Cellardyke's almost parallel main streets, East Forth Street and George Street, run towards the Union Harbour completed in 1867.

The heart of old Anstruther, the parish church of Anstruther Wester stands by the Dreel Burn on the site of the church of St Nicholas, said to have been consecrated in 1243. The church's salmon weathervane recalls Anstruther's long association with the fish trade. Next to the church is the old Town Hall fronting High Street with its many interesting crowstepped and pantiled town houses; today the old Town Hall is used by the Anstruther Improvement Association.

These days the fishing boats have gone and pleasure craft bob at anchor. The two main streets are linked by the Tolbooth donated by David Fowler and Stephen Williamson (once MP for the old constituency of St Andrews Burghs) in 1887; below their dedication panel is the iron-clamped old cross of Kilrenny dated 1642.

Along the road past the harbour, Cellardyke's bathing pool lies at Cardinal Steps. Happily the Scottish Development Agency have declared the coast towards the old mansion of Caiplie, once a secondary seat of the Anstruthers of Balcaskie, a Land Renewal Project. The Cardinal Steps take their name from Cardinal David Beaton who had a now-vanished residence overlooking the sea here. The pool, carved out of the natural rock, is where Beaton's episcopal barge was moored. At the top of the steps a pillar and ball memorial commemorates the Kilrenny men killed on land and sea during World War I.

Caiplie Caves are worthy of mention too, taking their name from a long disappeared Iron Age settlement; once used by St Adrian and St Ethernan as a retreat, the caves display prehistoric and early Christian inscriptions. An interesting tourist attraction is the arrival of the 'Sea Queen' at Cellardyke by boat from Anstruther. Taking place in August, this festival recalls when the sea was petitioned all along this coast from the 16th century for bounteous harvests. St Monans also had a sea-harvest thanksgiving.

For a thousand years the Isle of May, some four and a half miles across the Forth from Cellardyke, has been a retreat from the world. It was inhabited from Pictish times by hermits but was settled in earnest by St Adrian, first Bishop of St Andrews, in the days of King Kenneth MacAlpin. Adrian fell with Danish steel between his ribs on Holy Thursday 870, and sanctified the soil of May with his holy bones. The Rev Alban Butler's *Lives of the Saints* records: 'A great monastery was built of polished stone, in honour of St Adrian . . . the church of which, enriched by his relics, was a place of great devotion'. David I, however, founded the first really attestable religious community on the Isle of May around 1153, whose house was granted to the Benedictine Abbey of Reading, Berkshire. Indeed it was a house with far-flung lands from Pittenweem to Berwick-upon-Tweed. Interest in the island waned in the early 14th century and attention was centered on the Priory of Pittenweem, which had been established as a haven from Norse raiders centuries earlier; the possessions of May passed to the Augustinian Priory of St Andrews and by 1549 the ecclesiastical buildings on May were lying in waste and have now disappeared, although a small 13th-century chapel remains. The island was leased in 1549 to Patrick Learmonth of Dairsie, Provost of St Andrews, and subsequently had several owners like the Forrets of Fingask and the Lamonds of St Monans. Until, in 1815, the Northern Lighthouse Commissioners bought it for £60,000 from the Duchess of Portland, whose father General Scot of Balcomie had owned it from 1766.

Pictish beacons were precursors of a coal-fired lighthouse built here in a 45ft-tower in 1635-36. Twopence per ton was charged for ships passing the island. In 1816 the Northern Lighthouse board laid the foundation for a new lighthouse by

Robert Stevenson, with oil lamp and reflector. This lasted up to 1843 when Sir David Brewster's new dioptric lighting was incorporated; the lighthouse went electric in 1886.

Today, the Isle of May remains plain and flat, as its Celtic name *math* would suggest. The Midlothian Ornitholigical Club established a bird observatory here in 1934, although a serious study of migratory birds had begun in 1907. The whole island is now a Nature Reserve, the haunt of seabirds from guillemots to puffins and from cormorants to eider ducks, and is the last landfall for a multitude of birds on their migratory passage south.

Five wells still remain on the island: The Lady's Well was associated with St Thenew, who gave her name to the nearby Maiden Rocks. The Pilgrim's Well was the watering place of Pilgrim's Haven, where the devout disembarked on their holy way to seek the solace of Adrian's bones. St John's Well lies near the site of the priory, St Adrian's Well near the Alterstanes, and Sheep Well is named after animals which perished in its depths. The island is reached by a regular summer boat service from Anstruther.

Modern Anstruther is divided into two, Easter and Wester, by the Dreel Burn. Past the long curve of Edwardian houses, the A917 from Crail sweeps past Cunzie House (by the filling station). Here Robert Louis Stevenson spent some time in 1868, ostensibly to help his father who had been put in charge of the Union Harbour scheme at Cellardyke. In 'Random Memories' from *Across the Plains* (1892) RLS says, 'he lodged with Baillie Brown in a room filled with rose-leaves'; Brown was a carpenter by trade and was vouchsafed young RLS's secret 'I came as a young man to glean engineering experience from the building of the breakwater. But, indeed I had already my own private determination to be an author . . . Though I haunted the breakwater by day . . . my only industry was in the hours when I was not on duty! In the evenings RLS wrote *Voces Fidelium,* his dramatic verse dialogues. A verse of his is now weathering to extinction on the plaque of Cunzie House:

> Not one quick beat of your warm heart,
> Nor thought that came to you apart,
> Pleasure not pity, love nor pain
> Nor sorrow has gone by in vain.

Stevenson also strolled across the road to the aptly named Burial Brae leading to Anstruther Easter's parish church. The T-plan kirk is dated 1634 by the door and was dedicated to St Adrian. On the south wall of the church is the memorial of 1898 which contains the longest epitaph word in Europe, Tetuanireiaiteraiatea, which translates as 'The great God whose power extends to the heaven of heavens'. Such was the cognomen of Princess Tetuane Marama of Tahiti who married George Dairsie of Anstruther. She lived near the top of Kirk Wynd in Johnstone Lodge, which was converted into flats by the National Trust for Scotland.

Abutting the church is Anstruther Town Hall, a fine centrepiece for a characterful area of two-storey dwellings and narrow streets. School Green and High Street, with its Masonic Temple, impart the flavour of the past. In High Street was born William Tennant (1784-1848) in a narrow building next door to a tavern known as the 'Smuggler's Howff': the house was demolished in the 19th century, but the site is marked by a blue plaque. Tennant, later Professor of Oriental Languages at St Andrews, was a schoolmaster at Anstruther. He wrote *Anster Fair* (1812), a long poem on the courting of one Maggie Lauder who lived on the town's East Green in the 16th century. Tennant is buried at St Adrian's church where his inscribed obelisk is near the north-east corner of the church.

Past the church, along School Green, is Melville's Manse, said to be the oldest manse still occupied in Scotland. James Melville (1556-1614), whose *Autobiography and Diary* is a valuable account of his ministry at Anstruther, was the nephew of the famous founder of Scottish Presbyterianism, Andrew Melville (1545-1622). Melville began to construct his manse in 1590 when the area was part of Kilrenny. The story is still remembered how Melville acted as a negotiator when survivors of the Spanish Armada supply ship *El Gran Grifon* arrived at Anstruther on 6 December 1588. One of the Spanish grandees, General Don Juan Gomez de Medina, came ashore with his retinue and explained what had befallen the Spanish fleet; de Medina had himself been wrecked on Fair Isle and made passage in a hired ship to Anstruther.

The Anstruther folk gave sincere hospitality to the Spaniards which was to be repaid in a fortuitous way. On his way home de

A record crowd turned up at Pittenweem's Gala Day in 1978. Pittenweem, the home of the East Neuk fishing fleet, has been a royal burgh since the 16th century and was the site of a celebrated priory whose ruins and the neighbouring High Street are linked to the harbour by narrow wynds that run steeply to the quay walls. No other town on the East Neuk coast displays as much bustle and colour of the fishing industry as Pittenweem whose fish market is celebrated all over the country *(D.C. Thomson & Co Ltd)*.

Medina called in at Cadiz where he found a shipwrecked Anstruther fishing crew impounded by the authorities. The Commander pleaded the case of the Anstruther fishermen to the Spanish king and obtained their release.

Anstruther has had its share of idiosyncratic visitors. In 1779 John Paul Jones sailed threateningly up the Firth of Forth bent on buccaneering mischief. Thinking that Jones's ships were his own returning from Africa, Sir John Anstruther sent out a basket of vegetables and a packet of newspapers. Local worthies set out too, to greet the ships. Yet, only the pilot, Andrew Paton, was allowed aboard. Local stories conflict about the incident: some say that Jones opened fire on the 'guidfolk o' Anster'; others that he gave them powder, but no shot, to defend themselves against him! Such legends are fashioned to the liking of the teller.

Modern Anstruther is best assessed by an expedition on foot. A car park is located by the tidal harbour along from which is the lifeboat shed housing the 37ft self-righting Oakley-type lifeboat *The Doctors*. The North Carr Lightship nearby is now permanently moored as a maritime antique, across from the Scottish Fisheries Museum where the visitor can really taste the salty essence of Anstruther. The Museum was opened in July 1969 at St Ayles on the harbourside. Fish-dealing has been conducted on the site since 1318 when a land charter and fish market rights were granted by the Norman de Candelas to the monks of Balmerino Abbey. Thereafter a community of fishermen, brewers, coopers and salt dealers settled nearby; their spiritual needs were catered for by St Ayles Chapel, built in the 15th century, whose window-head is still preserved. Today the oldest building on the museum site is the accommodation for the representatives of Balmerino Abbey, now restored and colloquially known as 'Abbot's Lodging'. The museum presenting a panoramic history of the fishing communities of Scotland, is strewn with nautical ephemera, has a sea-water aquarium, and recreates a net-loft and a fisher-family room of around 1900.

Originally called Kinstrother, 'end of the marsh', and a Royal Burgh from 1587, Anstruther was until the 1940s the capital of the herring fishing industry in Scotland during the winter months. Rich shoals of herring arrived in the waters of the Forth annually and the fishermen of Scotland based themselves at Anstruther in January and remained until March. The shoals deserted their traditional waters in World War II. Once it was said that it was possible to walk from one side of the Dutch-influenced Anstruther harbour to the other by stepping from boat to boat. The inshore fishing continues with lemon sole, haddock and whiting, and the modern fad of scampi, formerly thrown away as worthless.

Anstruther once had its anti-pirate squad, and was a rich recruiting ground for the Press Gangs of the Royal Navy. Records show that Anstruther sailors played a vital part in the victory over the Dutch fleet at the Battle of Copenhagen in 1801, during the first war with Napoleon.

Along the harbour by Shore Street the merchants' houses still stand, and the old buildings have been restored to retain their historical appearance. Opposite the old Murray Library (1908) is the Burgh Cross. Standing some 9ft high, only the shaft is original, dating from 1677. Further along, on the gable end of a shop, is an inset of 1885 showing the carefully preserved masonic tools of the Lodge St Ayles No 95. Shore Streets runs into Rodger Street, and across the crossroads in St Andrews Street lies Waid Academy. Lt Andrew Waid left money in 1804 to found the school which provides secondary education for the district: the school entered the county system in 1921 and now incorporates a leisure centre.

The old folk still talk of 'Anster lore'. Fiercely superstitious, the fishermen saw bad luck in meeting a clergyman, a rat, a pig, or a salmon near a fishing boat; especially when encountering these before a fishing trip. Even the common names for these were taboo language. So a clergyman was referred to as 'the fellow with the white throat', a pig as 'a curlytail', and a salmon as 'the silver beastie'. Women have long been thought profane aboard a work ship; except on such occasions as the choosing of the Sea Queen. Then the fishermen reverted to the prehistoric race memory of petitioning a female shaman.

Out of Castle Street runs Wightman's Wynd, a narrow, dank passage jostling the site of the Castle of Dreel, built by the time of Robert I's rule. The 'dumbell' loop in the wall is considered to be a fragment of the old fortess. The Wynd emerges near the Post Office Close a stone's throw from the birthplace of Thomas Chalmers (1780-1847), the first Moderator of the Assembly of the Free Church of Scotland. His memory is kept alive by the Chalmers Memorial Church and the lighthouse at the end of the pier.

Round into Crail Road the way leads past the Smugglers Inn where Jacobite conspirators met during the 1715 rebellion. In the town archives was a letter written on behalf of Charles Edward Stuart's secretary, James Murray of Broughton, thanking Anstruther folk for quartering his troops in 1745. The road now runs sharply across the Dreel bridge. In the 16th century the bridge was of wood, but it was rebuilt in 1795 and has seen much service since. The bridge brings the visitor to Elizabeth Place and into Anstruther Wester. At the corner, on the left, is St Nicholas' church with its 16-century tower. St Ethernan founded a church here in the 7th century dedicated to St Adrian. The site was dedicated to St Nicholas, patron of the sea, in 1243. Here John Knox preached destruction and the last vestiges of popery were swept away. According to tradition St Nicholas' tower carried the first landward sea beacon ever lit in Fife.

Next to the church is the old Town Hall of Anstruther Wester. Running along its side is a road to the Esplanade and leading to the old manse of 1703, and a delightful walk which gives different views of the Anstruther scene. A walk on to the rock known as 'Johnny Doo's Pulpit', near Billowness bathing pool, recalls the legend of how Thomas Chalmers practised his sermons here.

Back by the church, where Elizabeth Place meets the High Street, is Buckie House, which is a recent reconstruction by the National Trust for Scotland. On the west end of the house can be seen the shellwork of the town worthy Alexander Batchelor, who died in 1866. The National Trust have combined Buckie House with the 18th-century property next door. Across the way a blue plaque marks the home of Captain John Keay who won fame as master of the tea-clipper *Ariel,* which held the all-time record of 83 days from Gravesend to Hong Kong on the famous China Run. *Ariel's* great rival was Captain McKinnon on the *Taeping,* owned by Alexander Roger of Cellardyke.

Past Buckie House is the 16th-century Dreel Tavern with a plaque which reads: 'James V, 1513-42, travelled incognito through Fife as the "Guid Man O'Ballengiech", coming to the Dreel Burn and fearful of wetting his hose, he was carried across at this point by a stout gaberlunzie woman, who was rewarded with the King's Purse'. 'Gaberlunzie' is an old Scots word meaning tramp or beggar.

Up the road from the Dreel Tavern is the Craw's Nest Hotel

St Monans once led the field as a fishing port where boats have been built since 1747. By the shore on the west edge of the town stands the unusual fishermen's church built by David II in the 1360s abutting the site of an older chapel near to the shrine of the Irish missionary St Monan set by the Inverie Burn. This notable Victorian photograph shows the church which still displays a large model of a sailing ship suspended from the roof of the transept *(St Andrews Preservation Trust)*.

whose name recalls a visit by Charles II. When entertained by Sir Philip Anstruther, the king remarked: 'Such a fine supper I have gotten in a craw's nest'. Charles was referring to a meal taken in a lofty tower room at Dreel Castle. The hotel was the former manse of Anstruther Wester which was sold after the two parish churches were united in 1961. Anstruther has long been famous for its hospitality and generosity, although the Regency club known as The Beggars' Benison, which continued until 1836, was a bawdy, self-indulgent institution which met in the disreputable hostelry in Card's Wynd. Today Anstruther folk channel their hospitality into their new main industry of tourism which has brought benefits to all the East Neuk coastal villages. Pittenweem is another such modern beneficiary.

A town of Flemish gables and designs, Pittenweem, from *pit* meaning farm and *uamh* meaning cave, is proud to tell its visitors on the road signs that it is the 'East Neuk Fishing Centre'. Indeed all the narrow streets lead to the steep inclines down to the harbour. Yet for the visitor the basic tone of Pittenweem is at first ecclesiastical. The two houses which stand out as the A917 snakes into the town are modern 'holy' places. On the left is the Church of Scotland manse built in 1838, while on the right is the Roman Catholic Church and Presbytery of Christ the King, supporting above its door a sculpture by the craftsman Sir Robert Lorimer.

The street names reflect Pittenweem's religious past, like Marygate and Abbey Wall Road, and the visitor cannot but notice the great sacerdotal heart of the town. Off Marygate, down by the old folks' cottages by Priory Court, past the Episcopal church of John the Evangelist lies the fine old priory gateway. Here was sited the 1318 Benedictine priory before it was transferred to the Isle of May. In 1472 the foundation became dependant on the Augustinians of St Andrews.

Today the Great House of the priory stands as a fine piece of renovation. Within the priory grounds were enacted the great cruelties against local 'witches'. In no other place in Scotland were witches hunted with such fervour as in Pittenweem. Rough justice was meted out with great gusto; Pittenweem folk were witch-hunting with diligence up to 1705.

At the end of Marygate, Routine Row branches off; at the

corner of the Row the yellow-painted house bears a shield-plaque of unusual interest. It tells how near the site the Kirkcaldy exciseman James Stark was robbed by two men, Andrew Wilson and Geordie Robertson, in 1736. At their subsequent trial in Edinburgh, their courage and demeanour won popular admiration and, their attempted escape while on their way to execution gave rise to the famous Porteous Riots immortalised by Sir Walter Scott in *The Heart of Midlothian.*

Across the road is the Kirk of Pittenweem (1588), nestling alongside the distinctive burgh tower with its old lock-up at the foot; along from the barred window stands the Town Cross, and although the capital of the Cross bears the date 1711, it is likely that the shaft is 16th-century. The church, once dedicated to St Adrian, has been totally restored, but stands on the site of the old priory church. In the graveyard are many interesting stones. Here lie the Hendersons of the Henderson Shipping Line, and one John Smith, the 18th-century horologist who made the church clock.

From the church the High Street leads to the modern shopping centre, and this thoroughfare presents a great mixture of architecture. The property of Adamson the baker (once the site of Pittenweem manse) and Bowman the fruiterer is dated 1635; next door is the distinctive Kellie Lodge, the 16th-century town house of the Earls of Kellie. The other way from the church, which skirts the site of the old priory land, is the steep cove Wynd which leads to St Fillan's cave and the harbour. St Fillan's cave, in the care of the Episcopal church, is well worth a visit. Legend has it that the 6th-century Fillan of Glendochart lived in the cave during his mission to the early dwellers of the East Neuk.

Pittenweem harbour was in ruins by the 16th century, but was repaired in 1687, and around it houses were established by brewers, shipbuilders, fishermen, tobacco merchants and ship masters. Most of the harbour house-facings today date from the 19th century. The harbour is the commercial heart of Pittenweem, with its covered fish market (1954) under the watchful eye of the Fishermens' Mutual Association, and not forgetting the hoary experience of the members of the Old Men's Club. At the harbour breakwater The Gyles is a 17th-century house owned by the other Captain James Cook, the one who took Charles II to France after the Battle of Worcester in 1651. The harbour strand leads to the colourful cottages of the West Shore. Here and there the peeling noticeboards tell that Pittenweem was once a Royal Burgh (1542), and the boards themselves are relics of past days of proud civic independence. Such alleys as Calman's Wynd, by the harbour, lead up to sheltered entries and quiet squares. Apart from street names like Waggon Road, there are no signs now of the flourishing coal trade Pittenweem once had.

Pittenweem's general market was justifiably famous, particularly the fairs of Ladyday (26 March) for linseed and shoes; Lammas (1 August, also known locally as Gooseberry Market) for wool; and Martinmas (11 November) for cattle. Today fish and tourism are the financial interests of Pittenweem.

North of Pittenweem, past the 18th-century Anchor Inn with its distinctive red and green marine lamps for port and starboard, and the old railway station site, lies Grangemuir House in the centre of the Prior of St Andrews' ancient hunting grounds. Built by Robert Bruce of Grangemuir around 1807, the house was enlarged in the 1870s by Lord William Keith Douglas. Once in the ownership of the Erskines of Cambo, the property was bought in 1974 and was subsequently developed as a caravan and chalet site with the name of Grangemuir Woodland Park. On the road out of Pittenweem the Eight Gables Hotel was once the distinctive mansion built in 1902 from the estate of an eccentric tobacco-chewing Australian, and has been an old people's home and a manse. Chesterhill House was once the home of the 19th-century Fife biographer, M.F. Conolly.

Formerly known as Abercrombie, which is in reality today a small village a mile or so away, St Monans lies between the Dreel Burn and St Monans Burn. Folklorists note that St Monans was one of the most superstitious villages of the East Neuk, which glorified in its isolation. Even now the visitor has to turn off the A917 to make a positive and much recommended visit to the village. Station Road, which leads to the two-basin harbour, cuts across the old railway line.

A burgh of barony since 1621, St Monans depended upon the fish trade for its prosperity, and the sea is still writ large in

In 1771 Lady Anne Lindsay (1750-1825), daughter of the Earl of Balcarres, wrote the very popular ballad *Auld Robin Gray*. Gray had been a herd on the Balcarres estate and his cottage is still to be seen at Colinsburgh, the village founded in 1705 by Colin, 3rd Earl of Balcarres, for the soldiers in his disbanded Jacobite army. In reality Robin Gray lived in a now-vanished cottage deeper within Balcarres estate *(D.C. Thomson & Co Ltd).*

its lifestyle. The individuality of St Monans fishermen was seen in the 1860s and 1870s when they personally raised the finance to make considerable improvements to their harbour. Today that harbour rings to the industry of Messrs. J.N. Miller & Sons Ltd who have built boats here since 1779, although the Miller family had established themselves as boatbuilders in 1747. St Monans houses snuggle by the harbour and cling to the rocks above the strand which leads to Miller's other yard at East Shore via The Neuk.

At St Monans is evidence of the sensible coming together of the National Trust for Scotland and the pre-local government reorganisation Town Council who joined to restore houses; particularly worth noting in the East Neuk are the outside staircases of the fishing cottages, the finest one in St Monans being that next to the house called The Anchorage. Restoration is all around and the Dundee College of Art played a part in the reconstruction of East Street. The town has fewer hostelries per acre than other East Neuk communities, probably because it was 'dry' during 1900-47.

West Shore leads, via the new houses at Braehead, to Scotland's kirk 'closest to the sea'. Dedicated to Monan, the Irish missionary companion of Adrian of May, the church was founded in 1265-67 by Alan Durward, Earl of Atholl and Chief Justiciar, but was built in its present form in 1326 with monies donated by David II whose arrow wounds received at the Battle of Neville's Cross in 1346 were healed through prayer at the shrine of St Monan. That's just one of the tenacious local legends, but the kirk was once a Royal Votive Chapel in the gift of the monarchy until the 19th century.

The church would be better dedicated to a soldier saint, for it has fought the sea for nearly 800 years, was burned by the English in 1544, shaken by mines in 1944 and now contends with damp. The kirk, first used as a parish church in 1646, is very much a place of worship for Calvinist fisherfolk: their marks are everywhere in trenchant opposition to the relics of the Dominican friars who once intoned their divine offices here. The church was restored in 1828 and renovated in the 1960s to a modern clinically-bright state. Although the pre-Reformation altars were swept away, a trefoil sedilla and piscina remain on the south wall of the choir around which are set Twelve Consecreation Crosses, one for each Apostle. The north gallery holds the 'Sailors' Loft', and a full-rigged model ship of 1800 hangs from the ceiling by the south transept. St Monans' Cave, a stone's throw from the church, marks the old shrine and hermitage of the place.

A few hundred yards along the cliffs from the tryptych of cemetries, lie the remains of Newark Castle. Originally in the possession of the Sandilands family who became the Lords Abercrombie, the castle had one really distinguished owner. He was General David Leslie, first Lord Newark, who defeated the Marquis of Montrose at the Battle of Philiphaugh in 1645. Leslie's bones rested until 1828 in the choir of St Monans kirk when they were unceremoniousy thrown over the sea wall by the zealous renovators. Newark passed to the Anstruthers and then the Bairds of Elie and is now a lonely ruin above the Long Shank rocks. Within sight of Newark, between the farmyard and the sea, lies the almost vanished Ardross Castle, built by Sir William Dishington in 1370 when he was Sheriff of Fife and agent of David II for the building of St Monans church.

The tiny village of Abercrombie with its white harled cottages sits less than a mile north of St Monans. Abercrombie farm (1892) lies on the site of the old mansion which had been built by Richard Cocus in 1260. The date of the founding of Abercrombie chapel is not known, but by the mid-12th century it was in the hands of the monks of Dunfermline. It was consecreated by Bishop David de Bernham in 1247, but was deserted exactly 400 years later when the seat of the parish moved to St Monans. Long used as a burial place of the Abercrombies and their retainers, the chapel stands ruined in Balcaskie Wood.

Through the trees at the road-end at Abercrombie can be seen Balcaskie House. The shell of a house at Balcaskie was old when Sir William Bruce of Kinross rebuilt it in 1670. Today the house is an oblong block of three stories, reached by a long straight drive from the 18th-century gates. Bruce bought the property in 1665, and the house and lands of Balcaskie are traceable to Juan Cook's ownership charter of 1223; and probably Bruce's architectural teeth were really cut here before he went to restore and rebuild Holyrood Palace. Much work was done on Balcaskie and its policies in Victorian times, but today the New Zealand laburnums, the Indian strawberry and the petrified Roman emperors add ambience to a house that would be stark without them. It remains a treasurehouse of Reynolds, Gainsboroughs, antique bric-a-brac and Louis XIV chairs. Bruce sold the property in 1684, and it was purchased in 1698 by Sir Robert Anstruther, whose family has owned the property ever since. The Fife family of Anstruther of Dreel Castle having long flourished as powerful land and shipowners and have intermarried with many Lowland families.

Elie House lies on the east boundary of the twin royal burghs of Elie and Earlsferry, between Elie East Links and Kilconquhar Loch. It is a house worth noting for its architecture and its fascinating local stories. Today it represents an amalgam of styles, with a nucleus of an L-shaped towerhouse built by Sir William Anstruther in 1697: parts of this are still discernable to the north and west. In 1366 the lands hereabouts belonged to Andrew Anstruther and it is likely that he built a house of some sort, the foundations of which may still lie beneath the modern mansion. It is likely, too, that Sir William Bruce of Kinross had a hand in the house's design. Once Elie House's main entrance was at the west side (it is now located at the east) with a perron (an external stone staircase) leading to a beautiful statued garden, now swept away. The garden elevation was possibly completed by William Adam and there is still an Adam fireplace in the lounge. Around 1853 Elie House passed from the Anstruthers and William Baird, of the prominent coal and iron family, occupied it into the 20th century. It was then taken over by Sir Michael Nairn in 1924; on Sir Michael's death in 1954 the house and immediate policies were bought by the nuns of the order of the Convent of Marie Reparatrice founded in Paris and Strasbourg in 1855 by the Belgian widow, Baroness Emilie d'Hooghvorst. The nuns sold the convent in 1982 and the house is now a health farm; the old stable area is privately owned.

The bulk of the policies around Elie House still belong to the Nairn Estates, which promote forestry. To the right of the main drive up to Elie House stands a tall monument without inscription. On it, however, is a horse's-head plaque which gives rise to two local stories. The monument is said to mark the burial place of either a famous Elie racehorse or the favourite horse of a former lady of the manor. No-one knows now exactly which is correct.

Elie House and its occupants have added much to Fife and Scottish folklore. Take for instance the story of Lady Fall, who married Sir John Anstruther in 1750. Janet Fall was the second daughter of Charles Fall, Provost of Dunbar and descendant of the gipsy Faa's. She was the famous Jenny Faa' mentioned by Thomas Carlyle as being 'a coquette and a beauty'. The said Jenny was peeved at the presence of the poor hamlet of Balclevie, which stood to the north of Elie House. Her dissatisfactions may have arisen from the fact that the tinkers who dwelt therein reminded her of her own lowly birth. So she pestered her husband to have the hamlet raised to the ground

Daniel Defoe (1660-1731) based his famous character Robinson Crusoe on Alexander Selkirk, a native of Lower Largo. A statue of Robinson Crusoe stands in a niche in the wall of the dwelling in Lower Largo now on the site of the house where Selkirk was born in 1676. The hell-raising son of a shoemaker, Selkirk quarrelled with the captain of the ship in which he was sailing and was marooned on the uninhabited island of Juan Fernandez. Defoe published his book using Selkirk's adventures as inspiration in 1719, two years before Selkirk's death *(D.C. Thomson & Co Ltd)*.

'to improve the view'. This was carried out and the eviction of the inhabitants possibly inspired Sir Walter Scott to weave the actuality around the fictitious eviction of the gipsies from Derncleuch by the Laird of Ellangowan in *Guy Mannering* (1815). Local legend has it that a *spey-wifie* (fortuneteller) from the doomed hamlet cursed the Anstruthers (as Meg Merrilies cursed Ellangowan) and forecast that only six generations of the family would live in the house. The prognostication was proved true. Incidentally, the old ruin which can be seen on the approach road to Elie from St Monans is also connected with the haughty Janet. The ruin is called Lady's Tower. It was intended as a summerhouse, but was used as a dressing-room for Janet after sea-bathing. It is said that when she went bathing, a bellman went round Elie to warn the villagers to keep away.

Five linked roads lead together to make up the spine of modern Elie and Earlsferry. High Street, past the Victoria Hotel opposite the church, leads to Bank Street and into Links Place, with the Golf and Marine Hotels, into Williamsburgh and across the old German Wynd into Earlsferry High Street. A mile-long strip of coast used to be four separate communities: from east to west, Elie, Liberty, Williamsburgh, and Earlsferry. Since 1929, all four have been united as the burgh of Elie and Earlsferry – Elie for short.

Elie, which had its royal charter reconfirmed by James VI in 1589, began to develop as a middle-class holiday resort after the boatbuilding, the fishing and the weaving had died out. The High Street has a tree-lined square. Stenton Row and Rankeillour Street lead down to the harbour constructed in 1586. The houses along the bay at Elie have a high wall as a bulwark against the advancing tide. Spray lashes their windows during storms, and sand from the beach drifts along the gutters. Down The Toft in the lee of Wood Haven by the coastguard lookout, nestle the yachts of today's prosperous workers. Archibald House, at the end of The Terrace, once served as the coastguard station.

Standing at the centre of Elie is the old parish church, built by Sir William Scott of Ardross Castle between 1630-38; this was when the parish was formed and endowed out of the parish of Kilconquhar. The distinctive campanile was added by Sir John Anstruther in 1726. In the kirkyard is to be seen an interesting range of tombstones; one worth noting is to be found set in the east-end wall of the kirk dedicated to the second daughter of Thomas Turnbull of Bogmill. There is a lifesize skeleton, covered from breast to ankles in a scroll shroud. In South Street, which lies between High Street and the harbour, are some of Elie's finest houses, in this the oldest and once most important part of the town. The house called The Castle is a fine example of early 16th-century Scottish architecture. Originally L-shaped, the tower of the house dates from the 15th century. This was the town house of the Gourlays of Kincraig, whose lands stand further along the coast above Shell Bay. The Gourlays, who have been here since the days of William I, 'The Lion' (1143-1214), had a family tie with the Sharps, whose famous kinsman, archbishop James Sharp, was murdered at Magus Muir in 1679. In The Castle Margaret Sharp received the news of her father's assassination. As in all East Neuk towns, Elie is a warren of pends and closes and until 1882 most of the old houses had their own wells.

Opposite The Castle is a heavy timbered door, richly carved but worn by the salt winds and sand. This gave access to a saw-pit for the Memel wood (from Lithuania) which was unloaded at Elie Harbour. Farther west is the eye-catching entrance to Gillespie House. Above the doorway is a rich stone lintel (1682) bearing the marriage initials of its builders, Alexander Gillespie of Newton Rires and his spouse Christina Small. Once it was called The Torret, or Muckle Yett (ie, big gate) of an earlier house on the site, the residence of the Duke of York, who became James VII & II and who was Governor of Scotland, 1679-82.

West House brings South Street to a dignified end, and is probably of 17th-century workmanship; from here a delightful view of Elie's sickle-shaped bay may be seen and the bustle of the oil tankers in the Firth of Forth.

Earlsferry is a royal burgh of greater antiquity than Elie. Ferries to the Lothians, mostly to and from North Berwick and Dirleton, began a long time before their recognised foundation by Alexander II in 1223. Here, on the great circle of sand, the Danes landed in 1033. Above where the sea-swell batters the small islands of West Vows and Chapel Ness, at Earlsferry's western extremity, stand the remains of the hospice run by the Cistercian nuns of North Berwick whose benefactor was Duncan, Earl of Fife. Crossing the Forth, with its heavy seas and harr (mist) thickest off Earlsferry, was a perilous business in medieval times and the nuns set up lamps to guide the doughty travellers; their work is carried on today by the East Vows Beacon. Behind the chapel lie Earlsferry Links, on which golf has been played since the 16th century; 18 holes were set out in 1895. Beside them is The Grange, founded by the Cistercian nuns. The house passed into the hands of the Rev

Alexander Wood, son of the famous seaman Sir Andrew Wood. For many centuries the lairds of Grange maintained a dispute with local people on rights to the use of the links. Particularly out of step with his neighbours was Walter of Grange, a feverent Jacobite who assisted the Earl of Mar when he landed at 16th-century Elie harbour by way of prelude to the 1715 Jacobite rebellion. Over this land, too, trundled the waggons of the fish 'cadgers' bound for the Royal Palace of Falkland. Next to The Grange is Kincraig hill with its interesting caves of Devil, Doo' and Macduff. The last is reached by a delightful walk along the foot of Earlsferry Brae. Legend has it that Macduff, Thane of Fife, hid here while awaiting a ferry to flee from Macbeth. Modern Rires farm, between Balcarres and Flagstaff hill, has within its policies the site of Macduff's now-vanished East Neuk castle.

III. Kilconquhar – Newburn – Upper Largo – Lower Largo – New Gilston – Lundin Links

From Earlsferry the A917 leads past the rich pastureland and woodlands of Elie House and Broomlees to Kilconquhar. The village, pronounced 'Kinucher', stands on the shores of a lovely loch, the only loch in Fife's Lowlands, which, legend has it, was formed in 1624 after a storm blocked a natural drainage channel. Formerly the neighbouring villages of Barnyards and Kilconquhar were separate, but now they are one and their loch is the haunt of a fine variety of waterbirds. The village has recently been given a facelift and is now one of the prettiest in Scotland, the recipient of a 'Best Kept Village' award. Set on a knoll by the shores of the loch, the parish church was built in 1820-21 and its distinctive 80ft tower is a landmark. There was a church here as early as the 12th century which was in the care of the nuns of North Berwick. Some historians have opined that the name of the village comes from *Kil,* meaning cell, and Conquhar, the Latinised name of Connacher the Hermit. The oldest ecclesiastical relic is the fragment of a nave by the church filled with the tombs of the Earls of Lindsay and the Austruther-Thompsons. Opposite the church stands the early 18th-century Kinneucher Inn.

The fastest steam locomotive in Scotland, the 1937 A4 Class LNER *Union of South Africa* steams along the private railway at Lochty. The railway is to be found on the B940 (Cupar/Crail road) 7m west of Crail, and is open to visitors from June to September on Sunday afternoons. The Lochty Private Railway Co operates a steam-hauled passenger service over 1½m of track, and displays locomotives, shunter and passenger coaches *(D.C. Thomson & Co Ltd).*

The cottage of one Robin Grey stands near to Kilconquhar. He had been a herd at Balcarres estate and was immortalised by Lady Anne Lindsay in the ballad which Sir Walter Scott thought 'slightly improper'. The verses began:

> When the sheep are in the fauld, and the kye's come hame,
> When a' the weary world to rest is gane,
> The waes o'my heart fa' in showers frae my e'e,
> Unkent by my gudeman wha sleeps soundly by me.

To the east of the village lie Kilconquhar House and the remains of an earlier castle. The original castle was built in 1547 on the lands of Sir John Bellenden, Lord Justice Clerk in the reign of James V. It then passed to Sir John Carstairs in 1634, and until very recently the modern L-shaped house was the seat of the Earls of Lindsay. The castle was badly damaged by fire in 1978, but was restored as the centrepiece of an estate of multi-ownership holiday villas.

From Kilconquhar the A917 links with the A921 at Balchristie to cut through the pastureland of Drumeldrie and Newburn to Largo. Balchristie, the 'Town of the Christians' after a supposed Culdee chapel here, was once the hunting range of Malcolm Canmore, and via the monks of Dunfermline and the Duncans of Balchristie the estates descended to the Bairds of Elie. Today the whole area is a mixture of scattered farms and 19th-century mansion houses like Lahill House which belonged in an earlier form to Sir Andrew Wood of Largo, and then the Glasgow merchants the Rintouls. Nearby Coates House was the seat of the Beatons of Criech, and Sir John Leslie (1766-1832), professor of mathematics at Edinburgh. Charleton House, with its surrounding woods named after Boer townships, was built in 1759 by John Thomson and descended to the Anstruthers of Balcaskie. Additions were made to the house in 1832, and in 1906 when Col Anstruther covered the open areas and made the north entrance to the design of Robert Lorimer.

Westward towards Largo, the road passes through the now almost deserted parish of Newburn. Its decline was brought about by the drift of the rural population to the towns. Its ruined church was first erected by the monks of Dunfermline in 1166. Today its shell is a mausoleum for local families, and the stones around testify to the more prosperous days when the folk of Newburn engaged in milling, handloom weaving, shoemaking, quarrying and salmon fishing. In the west corner of the windblown graveyard lie the Lorimers, of whom the architect Sir Robert Lorimer (1864-1929) is the most famous. A new parish church was built in 1815. This parish was once the home of the 'Royal Cadger'. It was his duty to carry fish from Earlsferry to the Royal Palace of Falkland. In recompense for such duties he had a free house at Newburn with the right to graze a cow and a pig in the parish.

Housing developments are fast making Upper or Kirkton of Largo, Lower Largo and Lundin Links into a single entity. The old two-storied cottages, harled with red roofs, have given way to less picturesque slated modern dwellings. The Largo Stone (now in the churchyard) shows that this area once saw extensive

Celtic activity. But Largo first entered the historical records when it was given over to the monastery at North Berwick by Duncan, Earl of Fife, in the 12th century. Today Upper Largo is a pleasant rural community which has as its centrepiece the 12th-century kirk, enlarged in 1688 and 1817, and restored in 1894. Down its main artery, the A915, the coaches once came from St Andrews to Largo Pier to link with Newhaven. Largo's chief industry was formerly the manufacture of linen, and there were once extensive bleaching greens in the village.

Largo is said to have derived its name from the Gaelic *leargach* meaning a 'sunny seaward slope'. Undoubedly the most famous son of Upper Largo was Sir Andrew Wood (c.1460-1540), who became a merchant trader of the busy port of Leith.Wood has been dubbed 'the Scottish Nelson', and the exploits of his ship the *Yellow Carvel,* with its 500 crew and 50 guns, are legendary. In this ship Wood defeated the English fleet in the Forth in 1498. All that remains of his castle is Wood's Tower. After heavy rain a 'canal' which was constructed by him can still be traced from the tower in the orchard of old Largo House, through the park behind the manse (1760). Down this waterway Wood sailed from his home to church. Largo House is now a ruin, but a pair of Durham eagles are still spread-winged on the gateposts of the South Lodge. Here lived the Durhams of whom the first was Sir Alexander Durham, Lord Lyon King of Arms, who acquired the estate in 1659. The house, of which the shell only remains, was built by Robert Adam in 1750. After 1945 it was inhabited by the Polish Army and was de-roofed soon after they vacated it. North of the church is a range of houses known as Wood's hospital. The benefice of John Wood of Orky, the hospital was founded in 1665 and was rebuilt in 1830. Called Wood's Houses in modern times, the old hospital was developed into sheltered housing for the aged.

Upper Largo is still linked to the sea by a footpath known locally as 'The Serpentine'; this leads to Temple Hill, denoting that the lands hereabouts once belonged to the Knights Templar. Their lands included those of modern Strathairly House, the family home of the Briggs who bought it from the Lundins in 1789. Visitors to Lower Largo cannot miss the statuette to Alexander Selkirk (formerly Selcraig), who inspired

Daniel Defoe to write the great adventure story *The Life and Surprising Adventures of Robinson Crusoe* (1719). Dressed in the recognisable garb of Defoe's hero, the statuette marks the site of the home where Selkirk was born in 1676, and was set up by David Gillies of Cardy House in 1885. Selkirk was the hellraising son of a shoemaker who ran away to sea. His wildness led him to rebel against Captain Thomas Stradling of the vessel *Cinque Ports,* and Selkirk was placed ashore on the deserted island of Juan Fernandez. After four years Selkirk was rescued in 1709 by Captain Woodes Rodgers of *The Duke* and died a Royal Marine in 1721. Daniel Defoe (c.1660-1731) toured Fife as part of his promotion of the Act of Union and as a 'spy' for Robert Harley, Earl of Oxford and English Secretary of State, in 1706. In particular Defoe wrote of the Jacobite murmurings in the county and produced his remarks on Fife in his *A Tour through the Whole Island of Britain* (1724-27). Cardy House at Lower Largo was built by Alexander Selkirk's descendant, David Selkirk Gillies, in 1871. He had built a net factory at Largo in 1867 and his house, now packed with Victorian ephemera, is open to visiting parties by prior arrangement.

The Largoes remain popular with holidaymakers drawn by the crescent of the clean, safe sands of Largo Bay. Near the old harbour is the characterful area of Drummochy by the splendid, but now redundant, railway bridge (1856) across the Kiel Burn; hereabouts lived the flax spinners and the employees of the linseed oil mill. Also linked with the Largoes in past years is the village of New Gilston, three miles away; it was a community which once supported a school but no church. Now it is a tiny country hamlet of a few scattered houses in an area much depopulated. To the north are the remnant mining villages of Largoward, Lathones and Radernie. Coal from their defunct mines was once transported to the Royal Palace of Falkland. Here coal was still being hewn in the 1920s for mine owners like the Lindsays. Around, the landscape is still pitted with shafts and the weathering shale heaps. Between New Gilston and Largo stand the ruins of the castle of Pitcruvie in the delightful Kiel's Den. The 14th-century estate came into the Lindsay family in 1498 and the early 16th-century castle fell into disuse following the tenancy of James Watson, Provost of St Andrews, in the 17th century.

On the north side of Largo too is volcanic Norrie's Law with its defensive enclosures and settlements dating from the late 1st millennium BC at a height of 965ft. For generations the legend has been recounted of the treasure found here. In 1819 a tinker discovered a collection of fine silver vessels and jewellery; the items disappeared but later some other fine examples were discovered during excavation and are housed in the Royal Museum of Scotland in Edinburgh.

Lundin Links, dubbed by local hoteliers the 'Scottish Riviera', stands in the old parish of Largo. Further along the A915 and to the right stands the ruined Lundin Tower, all that remains of the Lundin estates founded by Philip de Lundin in the days of Malcolm IV (1153-65). The lands passed through the Erskines of Torry and the Wemysses in 1840 to the Gilmours of Montrave, but the associated mansion was demolished in 1876. Here too are the celebrated Druidic Lundin Links Standing Stones set within the golf course of the Ladies Golf Club. Today Lundin Links thrives on its holiday trade and its golf course which was first set out in 1868 and restructured in 1877.

IV. Colinsburgh – Arncroach – Carnbee – Lochty – Dunino – Cameron

Colinsburgh came into being in 1705 and was formerly known as Nether Rires, but was later named after Colin, 3rd Earl of Balcarres (1652-1722), an ardent Jacobite who went into exile with the Stuarts 1693-1700. When he returned to Balcarres he founded Colinsburgh as a hamlet of single-story homes for his disbanded soldiers. He was placed under a kind of house arrest after his dabbling in the 1715 rebellion. The village remains small and tranquil, with examples of the Victorian philanthropy and local independence engendered by the Presbyterian work ethic. A library was founded here by public subscription in 1899, and a church was erected in 1843 to be re-united with Kilconquhar in 1925. The Balcarres Arms hotel was once an important posting-house. Lathallan public school was founded here in 1930, but was moved to Montrose in 1949. Balcarres House lies to the north-west of Colinsburgh and was built by Secretary of State John Lindsay, Lord Menmuir, son of the Earl of Crawford, in 1595. The mansion is mainly 19th century but incorporates some 16th-century work which was old when Charles II was entertained here in 1651. The sundial at Balcarres is 17th century and was brought from Leuchars castle. Within the grounds, too, stands a roofless Renaissance chapel, long a vault for the Earls of Crawford and Balcarres. Perhaps the oldest Lindsay property which can be titled is still extant Balbuthie farm of 1456.

The neighbouring parish of Carnbee holds two small villages, those of Arncroach and Carnbee. A mile or two away are Gillingshill Reservoirs, a favourite resort for picnics. The villages are backed by the 557ft Kellie Law, and the modern lands of Carnbee were long owned by the Melvilles of Raith. Carnbee's old mansion house was demolished in 1813, and the church which was under the charge of the abbey of Dunfermline in medieval times, was rebuilt in 1793.

Some three miles NNW of Pittenweem, Kellie Castle is well signposted along the main roads which traverse the East Neuk, and offers a rare sight of an unspoilt 16-17th century laird's house. The castle, restored garden and some 16 acres of land were purchased in 1970 by the National Trust for Scotland, and the main contents were acquired 'for the nation' by the Secretary of State for Scotland who gave them into the care of the Trust. The estate began as a *messuage* in the 11th century held by the Saxon family of Seward and the oldest part of the extant castle is thought to date from 1360. The estate was held by the Oliphants for over 200 years when it was sold to the Erskines in 1613, who were to become the Earls of Mar and Kellie. The castle was given its present form around 1573-1605 when the original tower house was developed into the T-shaped building. The lands and castle of Kellie were dissociated in the late 18th century and there followed a period of neglect, ruin and virtual abandonment. In early Victorian times the whole deteriorated – for a while part of the castle was used as lodgings for the manager of the coalmine at Balcormo – but in 1876 a lease was granted to Professor James Allan Lorimer of Edinburgh. The Lorimers were associated with Kellie until the present day, having bought the castle in 1948. Members of the family restored its furnishings and fabric, using the talents of such as Sir Robert Lorimer, famed for his National War Memorial at Edinburgh Castle and the Thistle Chapel at the High Kirk of St Giles. The castle and gardens are open to the public at set times and the castle interior includes the Great Hall (now the Drawing Room), the Withdrawing Room (now a Dining Room) with its waterfall panels, kitchen, study, the Earl's Room, and Vine Room with its ceiling painting of Mount Olympus by the Dutch painter Jacob de Wet.

A few miles away at Lochty the Fife Railway Preservation Group run a private railway as a working Steam Railway Museum, open to the public in the summer. The Lochty private railway began in September 1966 when John Cameron of Lochty farm bought the famous steam locomotive *Union of South Africa* No 60009 from British Rail. This 1937 LNER locomotive, designed by Sir Nigel Gresley, became the star turn of the railway project. On Lochty farm there remained a ¾-mile stretch of railway from a farm siding at Knightswood, a remnant of the 15-mile long Lochty branch railway line which had been opened in 1898 to serve the farms and the pits in the area. More track was relaid using rail from Lochgelly colliery and the private railway was officially opened in 1967.

A neighbour of Lochty is the 14th-century estate of Pittarthie with its 17th-century ruined fortified house. The last family to actually live in the castle around 1700 seems to have been the original builders the Bruces; later the property passed to the Hannays of Kingsmuir. From Lochty the Scottish kings' hunting ground stretched to the sea. David II appointed *cunningares* (keepers of the rabbit warrens) and foresters to look after the wildlife hereabouts. James V conceded Kingsmuir house to Charles Murray for services rendered, and the estate survives, the surrounding pastureland still bearing the royal name.

Antiquarians still argue over the origin of the name of the ancient parish of Dunino, a derivation from *dunningheanach,* 'the hill of the daughters', is favoured as a nunnery was said to have been founded here, and the Priory of St Andrews owned land hereabouts in the 12th century. That Dunino was a Celtic community is further argued by those who suggest a Celtic translation of Dunino as 'Fort of the hill'. In the woods by Dunino Den is the 'Celtic pot hole' set on Bell Craig, locally associated with pagan worship and ritual atrocities, and below the aperture there is a 'Pictish cross' cut into the rock. Maybe there were Druids at Dunino, but the pot hole, the ritual sacrifice and the 'romantic sylvan location' smack of a Regency or early Victorian imagination. Undoubtedly there was a Celtic community of some sort near, for the church is neighbour to the site of a stone circle; and there are fragments of Celtic hewn stone in the walls scattered around. The church of Dunino was consecrated in 1240 by Bishop de Bernham and there has been continuous worship to the present day. A manse has stood on the site of the present building since 1564 and it was put into good order in 1780. Opposite the manse lies a katabatic garden in whose walls are bee-boles set with shelves for skeps.

The principal private estate of the parish is still Stravithie. On the secularisation of ecclesiastical properties in the 16th century, the lands fell to Margaret Erskine, the lady of Loch Leven, who became Mary Stuart's jailor in 1567; she gave the lands subsequently to her illegitimate son by James V, the Lord James Stewart, the famous Regent Moray. The Sprots are the family most recently associated with the estate, and in 1918 the Tory Sir Alexander Sprot created a sensation by unseating the famous Liberal Prime Minister H.H. Asquith.

West of Dunino lies the estate of Kinaldy which came into the possession of the Scoto-Norman Aytoun family around 1539. The Aytouns, members of whose family were Captains-General of Stirling Castle and sub-priors of St Andrews Cathedral Priory, owned properties from Kippo to Wilkeston, and from Carthurlie to Lochton. The prophetic Thomas the Rhymer wrote of them 'That none of woman born should succeed to the estates of Kinaldy and Kippo save of the Aytoun Blood'. Perhaps the most famous son of the house was Sir Robert Aytoun (1569-1638) who attached himself to the court of James VI & I, to whom he had addressed a Latin panegyric. In the royal service till his death, Aytoun's most famous verse was *Diophantus and Charidora.* Writing both in Latin and English, Aytoun wrote versus which begin:

> I do confess thee sweet, yet find
> Thee such an unthrift of thy sweets . . .

Kellie Castle, near Pittenweem, with its 16 acres of gardens, is administered by the National Trust for Scotland and offers visitors fine glimpses of 16th- and 17th-century domestic architecture. The oldest parts of the castle date from c.1360 and the property was owned by the Oliphant family for over 250 years, and then by the Earls of Mar and Kellie. It was restored some hundred years ago by Professor James Lorimer. Among the treasures of craftsmanship is notable plaster work and painted panelling *(D.C. Thomson & Co Ltd)*.

which Robert Burns reworked as:

> I do confess thou art sae fair
> I wad been o'er the lugs in love

– the latter for his entries in *The Scots Musical Museum* (1797-1803). Aytoun too worked on an old ballad which features in the controversial origins of Burns's reworked 'Auld Lang Syne' in 1788.

The Aytouns held the lands and castle of Kinaldy until the turn of the 18th century, after which it passed to the Monypennys, but the Aytouns were to maintain a presence when their descendant, Roger Sinclair on Inchdairnie, was elected MP for Kirkcaldy Burghs in the 19th century. In 1778 the property was acquired by Col Robert Patton (1742-1812) of the Honourable East India Company, who had been secretary to Warren Hastings, 'nabob' and Governor of Bengal. Patton became Governor of St Helena, and when he died the estate was bought by Alexander Purvis; the Purvis family held the property until 1966. The present house was built in 1839 and extended in 1854 from stones from the ancient Kinaldy castle whose foundations are under a nearby stockyard.

North-west of Kinaldy, and founded in 1645, the parish of Cameron remains in an area of dispersed farmsteads with, as its focal point, the reservoir which is a haunt of local anglers and birdwatchers.

> In a wee cot-house far across the muir,
> Where peeweeps, plovers, and whaups cry dreary,
> There lived an auld maid for mony lang years,
> Wham ne'er a wooer did e'er ca' "Dearie".
> A lanely lass was Kate Dalrymple,
> A thrifty quean was Kate Dalrymple;
> Nae music, exceptin' the clear burnie's wimple,
> Wae heard round the dwellin' o'Kate Dalrymple.

Thus the 'peasant poet and precentor' William Watt (1792-1859) celebrated the unattractive but hardworking spinster Kate Dalrymple who is thought to have lived in her 'cot-house' in Cameron parish by the 'wimple' of Cameron burn. Kate, it seems, was transformed from rags to riches by a legacy and took up residence, tradition has it, at 129 South Street, St Andrews. The songs says that she entered polite society and wed the 'sarkin weaver' Willie Speedyspool. Her cottage has now vanished from Cameron but a field still bears her name.

Once the lands around Cameron belonged to the Priory of St Andrews, but by the 16th century private estates like that of Feddinch had become established. Undoubtedly Lathockar has the most continuous proprietary history, being granted to Sir John de Wemyss of Rires in 1383. The old mansion of Lathockar is now ruined.

From Cameron the A915 makes a direct route into St Andrews.

CHAPTER 6

Fife's Shores of Tay

I. Tayport – Newport – Wormit – Gauldry – Balmerino – Creich – Brunton – Lindores Abbey

It is possible at low tide to explore the whole of Fife's Tay shore from Tayport to Newburgh, although the whole route could take 12-14 hours in one go; nevertheless, it is enjoyably walkable in sections, albeit slow. The A919 from St Andrews and the A92 from Cupar meet at St Michael's crossroads to join the B945 which is a good place to start a round tour of Fife's share of the Firth of Tay and its landward areas. From the old resting point at St Michael's, on the old coaching route, the B945 passes the old fever hospital, now renovated as the Pinewoods Hotel, via Vicarsford, recalling the passage of the priests on their way to Forgan church, to lead to Tayport, also named Ferry-Port-On-Craig. The northernmost town in Fife, Ferryport was erected into a Burgh of Barony by the 1598 charter of James VI in favour of Robert Durie of that Ilk as superior; but the little town has been known as Tayport since 1846. A ferry site was used here by Macduff, Thane of Fife, during his flight into English exile from Macbeth's castle of Dunsinane. There is a delightful local tale that when Macduff arrived at the ferry he found that he had no money, so he paid the boatman with bread, thus giving the ferry the soubriquet of 'Ferry of the Loaf'. By the 12th century a hospice and chapel for travellers had been built here and were run by the monks of Arbroath Abbey. A popular ferry with merchants and cattle drovers, it cost 'one penny Scots' for each person and horse to cross in 1474. By the 15th Century, too, the crossing to Angus was considered of such strategic importance as to warrant a castle for protection. In 1855 only fragments of the Z-plan castle remained and they were demolished to make way for the rapidly expanding burgh; the site of the castle is now Castle Cottage, Castle Road.

The old parish church in Castle Street was built in 1607 and restored in 1794 and 1825, and its spire still leans towards the church because of a weakness in the Scotscraig vault below. The parish developed as one of handloom weavers and jute spinners with salmon fishing and shipbuilding as lucrative additions. The town expanded from an early foundation in Dalgleish Street and Tay Street; the site of the old market cross is now preserved in the wall in Dalgleish Street opposite Market Place.

In 1846 the Edinburgh and Northern Railway Co bought the ferry rights and built Tayport harbour to accommodate the huge iron paddlesteamers which were fitted with rails for the carrying of loaded coal trucks across the Tay. A new harbour was constructed in 1851 and Tayport developed as a busy port for the handling of china clay, timber and esparto grass. Here too was a fleet of 'puffers' used to dredge mussels from the Tay. Out to sea still stands the old Pile Lighthouse, a distinctive superstructure on stilts, dating from 1848. Employment increased rapidly in Tayport in the 19th century with the opening of a sawmill in 1850, a cloth mill in 1865 and an engineering works by 1875; and before the railway bridge was built over the Tay the burgh flourished as a ferry travellers' facility for overnight accommodation. The truck ferry closed when the second railway bridge opened in 1887, but a passenger ferry remained; the ferryboat service ceased to run in 1939. Tayport railway closed to passengers in 1966. Tayport harbour, where the ships from Russia and the Baltic used to unload, is fast developing today as a centre for leisure craft, although greatly affected by the opening of the 1.4-mile long Tay Road Bridge in 1966, making access to the commercial heart of Dundee just a short car or bus ride away, Tayport still thrives, offering uncrowded sandy beaches for scenic walks. There is easy access from Tayport to the picnic areas and forest trails of the Nature Conservancy sites at Tentsmuir Point and Morton Lochs.

Rising above Tayport, Craig Law and Hare Law take in the Scotscraig estate which dates back to the 12th century, and was once owned by the murdered Archbishop James Sharp; a sundial of his day remains and his initials and arms are to be seen on a gateway. Various families have owned the estate from

The Tay ferry steamer *Scotscraig* at Craig Pier, Dundee on 16 September 1951, looking towards the Fife coast and its destination at Newport. Ferries have plied the Tay between Angus and Fife since medieval times the main links being Broughty Ferry to Tayport and Dundee to Newport. In the heyday of steam ferries hundreds of sightseers cruised the river as far as Perth via the piers of Balmerino and Newburgh. Ferries across the Tay ceased in 1966 with the building of the Tay Road Bridge *(D.C. Thomson & Co Ltd)*.

the de Quincys to Sir Michael Scott of Balwearie (father of 'the wizard': see page 00) and from the Duries to the Dalgleishes who built the present mansion house in 1807 and Scotscraig Mains in 1821 – they also built the road to Newport in 1830. Another owner, Vice-Admiral W.H. Maitland-Dougall, acquired the estate in 1845 and was responsible for the setting up of the present Scotscraig Golf Club which had been founded in 1817, and re-established in 1887. Hare Law is also known as Tower Hill after the watch tower rebuilt in 1815 to commemorate the victory over Napoleon at Waterloo. An unusual memorial is to be seen at the beginning of Tay Street. Here a council house bears a plaque commemorating the visit to Tayport in 1877 of American President Ulysses S. Grant who was here to view the ill-fated railway bridge. The housing scheme, named President Grant Place, is on the site of Tayport Railway Station.

The B945 enters Tayport as Queen Street and passes the present Burgh Chambers (now the District Council local office and the Library), the distinctive Roman Catholic Church (1939) of 'Our Lady Star of the Sea', and Queen Street Church (1843), built stone by stone by Tayport folk themselves. The main road leaves as Albert Street, the B946, to hug the shoreline of Newport and offers a panoramic view of Broughty Ferry castle – Partan-Craig in medieval times – and Dundee on the opposite shore. On the shoreline below the B946 at this point are the now disused East Lighthouse of 1832, built by Robert Stevenson who also designed the West Lighthouse in the same year. The arches of the Tay Road Bridge straddle the road as it curves into Newport.

Few houses were built at Newport-on-Tay before the establishment of the modern ferry service to Dundee in 1822, and thereafter it became a popular area with the 'jute barons' who built large grey sandstone houses along the rolling banks of the southern shores of the Tay. By the time the Tay reaches Newport, as the longest river in Scotland, it has travelled nearly 120 miles from its sources on the northern slopes of Ben Lui to form a two-mile wide firth at Dundee. Salmon fishing on the Tay was always a major industry and Newport folk had the right to fish the river. Newport earned its living initially from a ferry from at least the 12th century on the site once called Seamylnes with its protective chapel dedicated to St Thomas the Martyr of Canterbury. Possibly first administered by the monks of Arbroath Abbey, the ferry passed to one Alan Kynnaird of Naughton. By 1639 it was in municipal control, and for about 200 years pinnaces, yawls and row-boats plied the waters. In the 1820s a new pier was constructed at Newport from the designs of Scottish engineer and stonemason Thomas Telford (1757-1834) and the ferry service continued into the present century. The greater portion of Newport was built on Tayfield estate, which formed part of the old barony of Inverdovat. The name was changed in the 18th century to Tayfield and has been associated with the Berry family ever since the present mansion was remodelled in 1828. Other buildings worthy of note in Newport are Trinity Church (1881), the Blyth Memorial Hall (1876) and the mansion of Kinbrae (1872), built for Sir John Leng MP, proprietor of the

Dundee Advertiser. The earliest buildings in Newport include the old coaching inn, now the Newport Hotel (1806) in the High Street, and Castle Cottage (1812) in Newburgh Road.

Newport's close neighbour of Woodhaven was the northern starting point for the coach across Fife to Pettycur (see page 00). Recognised in 1669 as a public ferry, Woodhaven pier was until the mid-19th century the most important of the south Tay ferries. Here in 1715 Rob Roy MacGregor crossed the Tay with his marauding horde. During his tour of Scotland in 1773 with James Boswell, Dr Samuel Johnson crossed the Tay from Woodhaven and complained: 'Though the water was not wide we paid four shillings'. Here too during World War II the Catalina and Sunderland flying boats of the No 333 Norwegian squadron were serviced; a memorial by the Wormit Boating Club marks the visit by King Haakon VII to the flying boats in 1944.

From 1869 until 1929 the training ship the *Mars* was a familiar sight moored off Woodhaven. *TTS Mars* was built as an 80-gun warship of the Royal Navy in 1848. After service in the Crimean War, the vessel was refitted as an industrial training ship. *Mars* was brought to the Tay in 1869 and became the home for 400 boys between the ages of 12 and 16. On board they were given a basic education, with training in seamanship, woodwork and tailoring, with emphasis too on rowing, boxing, swimming and gymnastics. Many of the boys came to the *Mars* on a naval scholarship to learn the basics of a sea career, while others were there because they were orphaned or homeless, or had committed civil misdemeanours or persistent truancy. In all some 7000 boys passed through training on the *Mars,* but by 1929 numbers had fallen off. *Mars* was then towed to Inverkeithing for breaking. The *Mars* was known for its band and choir and the boys served aboard a rescue vessel for the Tay. Woodhaven's old granary by the shore served as a hospital for the boys. Woodhaven pier is now the home of the Wormit Boating Club, and by the old boathouse (1799) is the Celtic cross memorial to the 'old boys' of the *Mars* who died in World War I.

Wormit owes its existence to the great Tay Railway Bridge which dominates the view here. There was a tiny hamlet around Scroggieside Farm before the site was chosen as the

Fife terminus for the bridge. It is said that Wormit was the first village in Scotland to have electric light, a facility introduced by one Alexander Stewart who built many of the Victorian houses here; power was generated by a windmill on Wormit Hill, supplemented by a steam engine which gave way to a coal-gas engine which chugged away until 1930. In 1854 Thomas Bouch, Manager and Engineer of the Edinburgh-Dundee railway, conceived the idea of building a bridge over the Tay and in 1871 the foundation stone was laid. In 1877 the first train crossed from Wormit to Dundee, but because of structural errors the bridge collapsed during the gale of 28 December 1879; as the spans of the bridge collapsed a train was crossing and it plunged into the Tay at a cost of 75 lives. In 1887 the new and more substantial bridge seen today was built to become the longest bridge in the UK.

Wormit station was opened in 1889 as a consequence of the Tay Bridge-Newport rail link of 1877-79, and was closed to passengers in 1969. The B946 sweeps past Wormit station site to join with the A914, but just at the edge of Wormit a minor road goes right to Balmerino past Naughton House. This is a part of the delightful Coastal Tourist Route to Newburgh and may be described as 'Fife's best kept secret', for the maze of often very narrow backroads leads to attractive valleys and hills, walks and vistas making for a charming day out.

The rich agricultural land of Balmerino lies mainly within the two old estates of Birkhill, with its 1859 baronial mansion incorporating one of 1780, and Naughton with its fine country mansion of 1793 built by James Morrison. Behind the house, on private land, is the site of Naughton Castle, reputed to have been first built in the 12th century by Robert de Lundin, the natural son of William I.

The hamlet of Balmerino owes its foundation to the Cistercian Abbey of St Edward the Confessor founded around 1227 by Ermengarde, widow of William the Lion. With its mother house at Melrose, Balmerino Abbey was built with stone from the nearby quarry at Hyrnside, and it is said the stone was transported on a specially dug canal. The abbey orchards were devastated in the gale of 1879 which destroyed the Tay Bridge. In time Queen Ermengarde was buried under the High Altar and her stone coffin was later used as an animal

Woodhaven quay looking towards Pluck the Crow Point and Newport-on-Tay. The village and pier of Woodhaven was the northern starting point for the coach route across Fife to Pettycur on the south shore of the county. The old granary building in the foreground once served as a hospital for boys from the *TTS Mars* and the old haven is now used as a marina for the local sailing club *(Peter Adamson)*.

trough. The abbey flourished until it was burned by the English in 1547 and despoiled by the Reformers in 1559. It was given over to Sir James Elphinstone, later Lord Balmerino, in 1603; his descendants, staunch Jacobites, ultimately forfeited the estate for their part in the Rebellion of 1745 and Arthur, the last Lord Balmerino, was executed for his pains. Today the abbey, with its picnic area, is in the care of the National Trust for Scotland to whom it was presented by the Earl of Dundee in 1936. A farmhouse was built in the cloister garth around 1849 and incorporates the monks' granary and doocot. A great and ancient Spanish chestnut tree near the site of the Abbot's House is pointed out as having been planted by the Cistercians. A walnut tree here too, not far from the site of the abbey's medieval orchards, is thought to have been planted by Mary Queen of Scots in 1565. The monks established a pier at

Balmerino for boats crossing the Tay, and this was used by paddlesteamers up to 1915; because of the ferry the abbey was on the 'pilgrimage route' to Arbroath and St Andrews. Balmerino Inn was long a popular rendezvous for excursionists from Dundee and dated from the 18th century. On the right as the visitor enters Balmerino is the memorial square of houses built after World War II by Henry Scrymgeour-Wedderburn, Hereditary Standard-bearer in Scotland, in memory of his brother killed at Anzio.

The hamlet of Gauldry, now a dormitory of Dundee and Cupar, is the largest community in Balmerino parish. It is served by two churches, one a former weaver's cottage within the village and the other at Bottomcraig dating from 1811, but altered in 1884. Today the old cottages which once housed weavers and estate workers are much sought after for renovation.

The back road from Balmerino, via Coultra and Hazelton Walls, leads to Creich and Brunton. The main feature of Creich is its hilltop woods with magnificent views, once the hunting grounds of the Earls of Fife. Its 14th-century church, with a 16th-century aisle, lies in ruin. Creich castle lies within a farmsteading and may be viewed from the approach road. There has been a castle here from at least the 13th century, but the 16th-century L-plan ruin is remembered particularly today for its occupancy by the Beatons of Balfour, hereditary Stewards of Fife. Mary Beaton of Creich was one of Mary Queen of Scots' 'four Maries'. The doocot of 1723 is still extant and Creich manse dates from 1816.

Brunton is a very scattered hamlet of narrow roads and cottages of mixed age and state of preservation, and at one time it had some of Scotland's tiniest farms, the result of feuing to tenants in the 18th century. Many of Brunton's old cottages had looms for the production of osnaburgs and dowlas, the coarse linen made from the locally grown blue-flowered flax. Stacked like corn, the flax piles were a common sight hereabouts, and up to the end of World War I it was harvested by women and children. Brunton with its long-closed meal mill and Free Church (1843) is truly a place where time has stood still.

Down from Creich towards the Tay lies the farmland that

makes up Flisk, all set within the policies of the 14th-15th century Ballinbreich Castle, the stronghold of the Leslies, Earls of Rothes. Visible from the roadside, the castle has a 14th-century keep with 16th-century additions. The Leslies of Ballinbreich, although hosts to Mary Queen of Scots during one of her visits to Fife, were implicated both in the murder of her secretary David Rizzio in 1566 and of her husband Henry Stewart, Lord Darnley, in 1567. Ballinbreich Castle was sold by the Leslies to finance the rebuilding of Leslie House which burned down in 1763. The rich land of Flisk supports cereals, vegetables and soft fruit, and the whinstone and lime steadings mostly date from the 18th-19th centuries. There was a parish school from 1873 to 1981, and the now roofless church was built here in 1790 on the site of a chapel consecrated in 1242. To the south lies the 850ft Norman's Law which the Norse invaders used as a burial ground.

From Flisk the back road skirts Lindores Hill to the left and descends to the ruins of Lindores Abbey scattered within the farm of Parkhill abutting the ancient port of Newburgh. Lindores Abbey was founded in 1191 by David, Earl of Huntingdon, for the Benedictine monks of the Order of Tiron, and it developed into one of the most celebrated of Scotland's religious settlements. At one time the abbey supported nine mills in the vicinity and established the thatching industry in Fife, utilising reeds from Lindores Loch and from the Tay. Here too the monks instituted fruit growing, from raspberry farms to pear and apple orchards.

Built of red and white sandstone the abbey, which had a mitred abbot, played a prominent part in the more notable events in Scottish history. Here Edward I demanded the allegiance of the lairds of North Fife, and maybe the famous Stone of Destiny, used for inaugurating Scottish Kings, and purloined from Scone Abbey near Perth in 1296, rested here on its journey to Westminster Abbey. Within the walls of Lindores Sir William Wallace celebrated the nearby Battle of Blackironside in 1298, when he defeated the Edwardian army of Sir John Seward. Here too was buried the Duke of Rothesay, James I's son and heir, mysteriously murdered at Falkland Place. The last Abbot of Lindores was John Lesley, Bishop of Ross, the faithful supporter of Mary Queen of Scots.

The Reformers sacked the abbey in 1543, expelling the monks; and in 1559 they returned to desecrate the altars, burn the books, manuscripts and vestments and despoil the tombs which included those, before the high altar of the three sons of the founder, Robert, Henry and John. Eventually the abbey was given over to Patrick Leslie, Lord Lindores, in 1600 and subsequently became a quarry for the local people; the practised eye can still detect fragments of Gothic doorways and windows incorporated in cottages and farms in the vicinity.

Today Lindores is a much neglected site worthy of future research, excavation and preservation. After all, Fife has too few monastic sites to allow this, one of the most important in Scotland, to be so badly ignored. Next to the abbey is Abbey House, built in 1872 on the site of an earlier edifice.

II. Newburgh – Abdie – Dunbog – Luthrie – Moonzie – Rathillet – Kilmany – Forgan

Newburgh lies on the A913 Perth-Cupar road and owed its foundation to the Abbey of Lindores. Probably originally a fishing village, this was erected into a *novo-burgus* by Alexander III in 1266 for the monks of Lindores. The area had been considered of great strategic importance by the Romans. Across the Fife/Perth boundary, within the private polices of Carpow House, is the site of a Roman fortress overlooking the junction of the rivers Earn and Tay, and the Carse of Gowrie. A good starting place to absorb something of the history of Newburgh's vicinity is to visit the Laing Museum in the High Street. It was first opened in 1896 as a gift of Dr Alexander Laing (1808-92), a banker and historian. His collection of antiques was amalgamated with the geological specimens of his uncle, the Rev Dr John Anderson (1796-1864), to form the basis of the modern collection. Laing made a special study of the Dark Age hill fort at Clatchard Craig, south-east of Newburgh, and promoted various local 'self-help' schemes so dear to the Victorian philanthropist. The museum display also outlines the exploration and settlement of the Pacific, as several of Laing's family emigrated to Australia and New Zealand and sent relics home.

A royal burgh confirmed in 1457, Newburgh is the only

Woodhaven pier was used during World War II to service the Catalina and Sunderland flying boats of No 333 Squadron of the Royal Norwegian Air Force. The plaque commemorates the visits of King Haakon VII of Norway (1872-1957). In April 1940 Norway had been invaded by Germany and King Haakon left the country not to return until 1945. Near to the Norwegian memorial is a granite cross in memory of the boys of the *Mars* who fell in World War I *(Peter Adamson).*

clearly developed town between Newport-on-Tay and Perth, and its buildings are mostly of the 18th and 19th centuries, ranging from its manse (c.1790) and George Hotel (1811) to St Katherine's Church (1833) and the Town House (1808). A living was formerly earned from fishing, agriculture, horticulture and weaving, and within more modern times at the Tayside Floorcloth Co (1896) which closed in 1978. In the heyday of the paddlesteamers on the Tay, hundreds of excursionists called at Taylor's and Rennie's town piers, and in 1846 the Edinburgh and Northern Railway opened a station. To the north-west of Newburgh the estate of Mugdrum came into the possession of the Orme familiy in the 16th century, having been a part of Abernethy church lands, and from them it passed to the Leslies, the Lords of Lindores. At one time it was the home of the Jacobite Lord George Murray, a distinguished leader of the 1745 rebellion. In 1794 the superiors became the Hays who held sway until the 20th century. Georgian Mugdrum House burned down in 1916. One of Newburgh's earliest relics is the Cross of Mugdrum (on private land), with its carved representation of the boar hunt, now set within the policies of Mugdrum House.

Another cross stood above Newburgh, on the hill to the south, and is thought to have been destroyed by the Reformers in 1559 because of its overt religious symbolism. Known as Macduff's Cross, it was regarded locally as a place of sanctuary for members of the Macduff clan; the forfeit for the privilege was the tethering of nine cattle to the nine rings the cross was once said to have sported. Only the base of the cross survives within a circle of marked stones.

Newburgh was once known for its fair on the Feast of St Katherine the Virgin and Martyr whose feast day was 25th November; this became known as the 'Haggis Fair' when its religious overtones were debunked. The fair survived into modern times. Up to 1900, too, the members of the Masonic Lodge held a torchlight procession in full regalia to mark the Festival of St John the Divine, the Apostle and Evangelist.

Bethune's Cottage, at the top of Hill Road, dating from 1837, but extended and improved, is of particular interest as the home of the two largely self-educated brothers, Alexander and John Bethume, who broke stones for the Newburgh road. Although Alexander became a cripple following a quarry explosion and John died in 1839 from privation and overwork, they are remembered as competent local poets. Indeed the Rev Charles Kingsley, of *Water Babies* fame, declared that their cottage should rival that of Robert Burns as a shrine. Alexander published his famous *Tales and Sketches of the Scottish Peasantry* and because of ill-health was unable to take up the proffered editorship of the *Dumfries Standard;* he died in 1843. The two brothers are buried in Abdie churchyard. Alexander Bethune's own musings make a fitting epitaph:

Well, be it so: methinks my life, though short,
Hath taught me that this sublunary world
Is something else than fancy wont to paint it –
A world of many cares and anxious thoughts,
Pains, sufferings, abstinence, and endless toil,
From which it were small penance to be gone.

The A913 to Cupar passes through the parish of Abdie, and to the right is the quarry which gave Newburgh folk employment, and opposite stands the ruins of the 15th-16th century Denmylne castle; an early fortress of the Earls of Fife stood here, after which the present castle was built by Alexander Balfour; it was abandoned when the policies were sold in 1772. A famous owner was Sir James Balfour of Kinnaird, Lord Lyon King of Arms, who, as a noted antiquarian, amassed a huge collection of historical manuscripts, many of which are now housed in the National Library of Scotland. He was also involved in the survey of the sheriffdom of Fife used by the cartographer Timothy Pont (see page 123).

At Den of Lindores the A983 links with Auchtermuchty and bypasses the old monastic farm sites of Grange of Lindores, Ormiston, Berryhill and Hilton. Down the A913 Lindores is the only village in Abdie parish, although the Priest's Burn, from Lindores Loch to the Tay, once supplied power for nine mills. Once too there were three lochs between Abdie Church and Dunbog, but Lindores is the only one remaining, although the 'bottomless' Black Loch and Red Myre on Weddersbie Hill are still close historic neighbours. Today Lindores Loch is the haunt of fly fishers. Within sight of the loch is the site of the now demolished Inchrye Abbey, a mansion of 1827, and Lindores House of 1820.

On the far shore of the loch lies Abdie church (1827) abutting the now ruined church of St Magridin, dedicated in 1242 and used until 1827. Within the churchyard is the memorial to Sir Frederick Lewis Maitland (1777-1839), captain of the British warship *HMS Bellerophon* which took the defeated Napoleon on board in 1815 and transferred him to the *Northumberland* which carried him into exile on St Helena. Rear-Admiral Maitland of Lindores House died in his ship off India. The Denmylne Aisle of 1661 is worthy of note, as is the

Pictish Symbol Stone which now stands in a stone shelter by the churchyard gate. The stone shows a mirror symbol – long the token of aristocracy amongst the Picts – on one side, and a cauldron device, a V-rod design and a carved crescent on another; at one time a thrifty Fifer carved a sundial on the stone which was once part of a nearby dyke. Among other tombstones is part of a defaced tomb effigy.

The sparsely populated parish of Dunbog comprises the two estates of Aytounhill and Zetland, of which the latter's mansion was built in 1660. Dunbog House was established around 1580, but it is much altered; the ruined 16th-century square keep of Collairnie Tower, home of the Barclays, lies towards the south-east. Mary Queen of Scots visited in 1564. The tiny hamlet of Glenduckie lies to the north of Dunbog and was within the hunting grounds of the Earls of Fife. Ayton's 17th-century chapel of Dundermore lies in ruins and Dunbog church of 1803 was altered in 1837 when a tower was added.

From Ayton there are fine walks to Norman's Law, vividly bright in April and June with the gorse at its best. It is well to note that this is private property, but the East Fife Ranger Service observes that walks may be taken at the owner's discretion by walkers who show consideration for animal life. From Ayton the back road leads to Luthrie, but it is best to reach the village by car down the A913, turning left onto the A914 at Parbroath crossroads.

At one time Luthrie station was the most important stop on the North British Railway's North Fife line. Closed to passengers in 1951, the station won its fame as a loading point for 4000 tons of potatoes annually. Up to the 16th century Luthrie belonged to the Crown, and thereafter properties here were owned by John Murray, barber-surgeon to James V. Both Luthrie and Parbroath mansions have disappeared, the latter once belonging to the Hopetoun estates; the Hopetoun monument (see page 99), which dominates the local landscape, perpetuates the family's memory.

A turn off the A914, past the medieval estate of Colluthie with its Victorian mansion, and into the parish of Moonzie is to be recommended. The first encounter with history hereabouts is the ruin of the late 15th-century rectangular keep of

The red freestone arch of the ruined parlour and slype of the Tironesian abbey of Lindores forms this Victorian pose of 1876 by W. Ballingall. Founded in 1191 by David, Earl of Huntingdon, the abbey was sacked by the Reformers in 1543 and 1559. From the 18th century it was used as a quarry by the local folk of Newburgh, and very little of the structure remains.

Lordscairnie Castle with the remains of its courtyard defences. Once the stronghold of the Earls of Lindsday, the castle was used as a church in 1688.

Moonzie's old church was immortalised in an old rhyme:

> Gae ye east, or gae ye west,
> Or gae ye ony way ye will,
> Ye winna get tae Moonzie Kirk
> Unless ye gae up Moonzie hill.

The random rubble church, with its once whitewashed east gable wall, was a landmark for sailors heading for St Andrews Bay, or for mariners of the Dundee Whaling Fleet making for the Tay. Dedicated to the Holy Trinity in 1245, Moonzie church was renovated in the 18th century and in 1882, and is in the care of a Preservation Trust which mounts displays of the parish muniments in July and August.

Back on the A914, the next hamlet encountered is Rathillet, an ancient property of the Earls of Fife. Both the estates of Rathillet and Moonzie supported religious foundations in medieval times; Rathillet funded the house of the Dominicans at Cupar, and Moonzie the Trinitarian hospital of St Mary at Scotlandwell, Kinross. Rathillet was the home of David Hackston, one of the Covenanting murderers of Archbishop James Sharp in 1679; Hackston heirs held the property until the 19th century. The United Free church of Rathillet was demolished recently to allow road repairs. To the north-west of Rathillet is Mountquhanie estate with its ruined 16th-century castle and mansion of 1820; Mountquhanie stables date from 1682 and 1811, and the icehouse is 19th century. Once belonging to the Earls of Fife, Mountquhanie became another Balfour property and was acquired by the Lumsdens; one famous scion of Mountquhanie was General Robert Lumsden who defended Dundee against General George Monck and Cromwell's army in 1651. When Dundee fell the general's head was fixed on a spike on the Old Steeple and there it remained well into the 18th century.

Next along the A914, which bypasses it, is Kilmany and its neighbour to the south, Logie, both set within agricultural hill country of distinctive beauty. Kilmany village has a number of interesting 19th-century cottages, while its church dates from 1768 and was originally a rectory granted to St Salvator's College, St Andrews by Bishop James Kennedy. One of the most famous ministers of Kilmany was the Rev Dr Thomas Chalmers who served here from 1803 to 1815. Buried in the churchyard is the Earl of Melville, one of the Scottish noblemen who supported William of Orange when he became joint-ruler with Mary II in 1689. Logie church, on a pre-Reformation site, dates from 1826 and is now the Elizabeth Sharp Memorial Hall. Logie House was built around 1750.

The late 15th/early 16th-century L-plan Cruivie Castle sits to the north of Logie on a rocky outcrop within a farm complex and on private land. The first castle on the site is thought to have been built by Sir John Wemyss of Leuchars. In time the Cruivie estates fell to the Earls of Southesk, but were forfeit after the Rebellion of 1715 and had several owners until the policies were merged with those of the Gillespies of

The Leng memorial chapel stands out above Vicarsford cemetery like a French mini-cathedral. Built by Sir John Leng, proprietor of the *Dundee Advertiser,* it is found near the busy A92 Cupar-Dundee road opposite Pickletillem. Nearby are located the ruins of the late 12th-century St Fillan's church, Forgan, disused since 1841; the church was modified in the late 16th century and stands near the remains of Kirkton House *(Peter Adamson).*

Mountquhanie.

The A914 passes Sandford at the junction with the B946. Alternatively named St Fort, Sandford was a Norman land portion, but it is better known today on account of the Sandford House Hotel, the converted dwelling of 1913 built by the architect Mackay Hugh Baillie Scott. The A914 joins the A92 from St Andrews, and a return to St Michael's crossroads down the A92 brings the visitor to Forgan. The church by the roadside, dating from 1841, is no longer used for religious purposes, and on the hill within Vicarsford cemetery is the memorial Gothic sanctuary built in 1897 by Sir John Leng (1828-1906) as a burial place for his family. Past this cemetery is the ruined T-shaped church of St Fillan. The church was founded in 1124 and was one of the gifts made by David I to the Priory of St Andrews. The church was extensively repaired in 1700 and 1770 when the Laird's Gallery was added; the church was replaced by the new one on land from the St Fort estates. In the graveyard of the old church lies the Stewarts of St Fort, and to the west of the ruin is that of the 16th-century three-storied Kirkton House. Morton House, across the B945 to Tayport, was first built in 1640 and remodelled in 1750.

The A92 continues, via Pickletillem – a curious name probably from *pette-talamh,* 'portion of fine land' – to the close of this tour at St Michael's.

Index